Mustard Doesn't Go on Corn!

How Respect, Openness, and a Simple Process
for Innovation Can Lead to Great Ideas

Richard Trombetta

authorHOUSE®

AuthorHouse™
1663 Liberty Drive
Bloomington, IN 47403
www.authorhouse.com
Phone: 1 (800) 839-8640

Published by AuthorHouse 11/08/2016

ISBN: 978-1-5246-4922-7 (sc)
ISBN: 978-1-5246-4921-0 (e)

Print information available on the last page.

This book is printed on acid-free paper.

I would like to dedicate this book to my wife who constantly encourages me to carry out my mission and to my daughters who never cease to teach me new and exciting things every day.

I would also like to dedicate this book to my parents, who continue to provide unconditional support despite their struggle to come up with an answer to the question 'what does Rich do?'

Table of Contents

Chapter 1

Innovation-What is it, why do we all want it so badly, and can it really be easy?

"We don't like their sound, and guitar music is on the way out."

—Decca Recording Co. rejecting the Beatles, 1962.

Imagine you are in 5th grade and, as part of a school project, you are given a large box of items and asked to build something. Pipe cleaners, pieces of wood, dowels, nails, glue, tape, straws, and fabric are just some of the materials that are contained in this box. There are probably about 30 items in all. In addition, you are encouraged to construct something on your own and, ideally, without parental involvement, and that has to do with the outdoors or the environment. The teachers will judge the projects and someone would be awarded first place. For what, we really have no idea. You get to work. Maybe you take out all of the materials and just start building. Maybe you sketch a plan. Maybe, if you are like my friend, Bob, you do something completely different. If you are like Bob you toss aside almost all of the items and keep only three that you have decided to use-a piece of wood, a nail, and a dowel. As the rest of us worked at building sail boats, camp sites, and model farms, Bob traveled a path that was so brilliant that it resulted in him being questioned at length-almost interrogated-by teachers and school administrators. Bob, completely on his own, built a sundial. How do I know he did this on his own? The dowel he used to was cracked where he hammered in the nail to attach it to the piece of wood. If an adult had helped him, I am confident that a pilot hole created with a drill to avoid cracking the dowel would have been the more expected approach. Also, the end of the dowel was not cut or sawed to make a smooth connection to the wood-another give away that Bob had done this on his own. Bob's sundial was so contrarian to what everyone else had done that teachers were actually puzzled. "Where did you come up with this idea?" "Who helped you?" "What did you do with the rest of the materials?" It was almost like watching Dustin Hoffman in the movie Marathon Man being asked over and over again, "is it safe?" While the rest of us stood proudly by our creations-I am not sure any of us followed the rule around parental involvement-Bob, being cornered by towering adults, kept his cool. "I saw this in Popular Mechanics. My Dad gets that at home." The interrogation stopped and the teachers convened about ten feet away from Bob to discuss the matter. Looking back at the situation it now seems similar to when there is a controversial call during a football game and the referees decide to do a video tape review, leaving us all waiting with anticipation as to if the call will stand or be overturned. After about two minutes, it happened. I can still see it as clear as day. Just like the football official who starts his sentence with "after reviewing the play..." one teacher made an announcement. "We are excited to award Bob first prize for his project." Gasp! Being a close friend of Bob's this was exciting and I was happy for him. However, for the rest of the class there was a collective "what just happened?" reaction that was a mix of confusion, anger, and sadness. The beautiful boats cut at precision angles. The cows made from pipe cleaners. The planes with propellers that spun. All of these lost to a sundial made with only three items, one of which was cracked in the building process. What Bob had done is what we will discuss in this book. He looked at something and, rather than go with complexity, he went for simplicity. He did not get constrained by traditional thinking, and, possibly most importantly, he lived in a household that fostered a culture of curiosity and positive reactions to ideas (I know this to be fact since I spent many days at his home building forts and eating peanut butter and jelly sandwiches). The culture in which he was raised encouraged this type of thinking-almost risk taking-when faced with problems. To

Bob, throwing out almost all of the items and taking about ten minutes to build his project (I believe mine took days) was not risky nor was it unconventional. It was normal. It was innovative. It was EASY.

IBM, in a recent annual Global CEO Study, states that "According to a major new IBM survey of more than 1,500 Chief Executive Officers from 60 countries and 33 industries worldwide, chief executives believe that—more than rigor, management discipline, integrity or even vision—successfully navigating an increasing complex world will require creativity." (IBM, 2011)[1] The study also found that "less than half of global CEOs believe their enterprises are adequately prepared to handle a highly volatile, increasingly complex business environment. CEOs are confronted with massive shifts-new government regulations, changes in global economic power centers, accelerated industry transformation, growing volumes of data, rapidly evolving customer preferences-that, according to the study, can be overcome by instilling "creativity" throughout an organization."

In addition, The Society of Human Resources Management (SHRM) reports that "As the global playing field becomes increasingly level, many business forecasters are predicting that workforce creativity and innovation will be the most important factors in establishing and maintaining a competitive advantage. Logic, linear thinking and rule-based analysis-functions located in the left side of the human brain-will remain important, but are no longer sufficient to succeed in the global economy. Many experts, such as author Daniel Pink believe that, to succeed, organizations must place greater emphasis on right-brain functions: artistic, big-picture thinking and the ability to put things in context." (SHRM, 2007)[2]

Finally, Price Waterhouse Coopers (PWC), conducted a similar study to IBM's in which "The results of [a] survey of 1,757 executives couldn't be clearer: innovation today is a key driver of organic growth for all companies—regardless of sector or geography. Meanwhile, innovation leaders are breaking away from their cohorts, expecting a revenue boost of a quarter-trillion US dollars over the next five years alone." (PWC, 2013)[3]

Ok, we all want 'it,' but what exactly is 'it,' with 'it' being innovation and 'its' close cousin, creativity?

In its purest form, innovation is defined by Merriam Webster as "a new idea, device, or method; the act or process of introducing new ideas, devices, or methods." From here, we are off to the races. As Maryfran Johnson wrote *Computerworld,*

"Everybody loves to talk about innovation, but try finding two people who can agree on exactly what it is. That was probably the case back in 1548 when the word first surfaced in the English language. Yet here we are, centuries later, still poking around on this eternal innovation quest."[4] Rather than spend the next 100 pages debating or attempting to accomplish the impossible-create the one and all encompassing definition of innovation-I will propose we start with Merriam Webster and toss in a tiny bit of additional verbiage:

> *Innovation is the creation of-and action upon-ideas to develop a new process, concept, or material object that solves a problem or addresses an apparent or latent need.*

It should be noted that there is a distinction between innovation and invention. David Nye, is his book, *Technology Matters-Questions to live with*, writes "Inventions are fundamental breakthroughs, and there have been relatively few."[5] Innovations, he argues, are "improvements on inventions." For example, he illustrates this point by showing how the incandescent electric light was an invention and that new kids of filaments were innovations.

There appears to be no shortage of courses, workshops, consultants, or books devoted to the topic of innovation. Just as with diets or personal finance, there seems to be an abundance of opinions and approaches on how to create an innovative company, yet, there are still so few organizations that would rate themselves on par with the likes of Apple or Google. Again, just like with losing weight or managing personal finance, becoming an innovative company seems difficult when, in actuality, it is quite easy. Yes, it is easy. Want to get out of debt? Spend less and save more. Want to lose weight? Eat less calories and exercise. Keeping with the diet and personal finance analogies, the key to becoming an innovative culture does not lie in complicated solutions, advanced degrees, elaborate scientific modeling or iPad apps. While an app may help one keep track of calories and performance, it can't stop one from eating a Twinkie (side note: I love Twinkies and it pains me to write that sentence). In terms of finance, if you have twenty dollars and a designer shirt costs thirty, well, maybe you need to put it back on the shelf. It doesn't take an advanced degree in mathematics to sort that one out. The same is true for innovation. While I have great respect for the tremendous work that has been done in this area-some of which will be used throughout this book-it is my experience that any initiative around innovation needs to me made as simple as possible in order for it to stick. It starts with a culture that promotes behaviors that foster respect and openness and ends with having a simple process that enables ideas to be shared, evaluated and acted upon. It is that easy. Really? That's "it?" Creating an innovative culture is that simple. How could this be?

This is the best part of this approach. It is simple. It is easy. I once had an engineering professor share something with me that I have never forgotten. He told me, "If you are struggling to solve a problem on an exam, immediately think of the most obvious and simple solution." I was confused. This went against conventional thinking that exams would be difficult and challenging. "Think of it this way," he said. "I have to correct over 100 exams, each containing page after page of mathematics and engineering principles. I design the answers to be things such as 'zero' or 'two times Pi,' not some complex value that would create headaches for me while grading a student's work. The problem may appear complex but the answer is usually quite simple." While the book and movie *Moneyball* have made baseball into a study in statistics and computer based analysis, it is difficult to argue with the 1988 movie, *Bull Durham*, when baseball is summarized in the following eighteen words: "This is a very simple game. You throw the ball, you catch the ball, you hit the ball." The same can be said for innovation. What may appear to be complex actually has a simple answer, and it is right here in this book.

Simple. Simple. Simple. As Leonardo da Vinci said, "Simplicity is the ultimate sophistication." When I worked at GE we lived by the mantra "Speed, simplicity, and self-confidence." Steve Jobs, a name synonymous with innovation, had a passion for innovation and for simplicity. As the headline of Apple's first marketing brochure proclaimed in 1977, "Simplicity is the ultimate sophistication."[6] (remember the da Vinci quote?) But the idea that innovation is easy is not my opinion, it is fact. Daniel Pink, in his book *Drive-The Surprising Truth About What Motivates Us*, writes "Too many organizations—not just companies, but governments and nonprofits as well— still operate from assumptions about human potential and individual performance that are outdated, unexamined, and rooted more in folklore than in science."[7] He adds "For too long, there's been a mismatch between what science knows and what business does." This book, like *Drive*, will not be based on assumptions or hunches. It will not be written with the perspective of 'trust me this approach works.' The idea that innovation is actually easy will be supported by scientific evidence and proof.

Example: Providence Talks

Betty Hart, Ph.D., and Todd R. Risley, Ph.D conducted a longitudinal study in which they analyzed parent-child talk, e.g. the verbal interactions between a parent(s) and his or her child. Their study had three key findings:

1. The variation in children's IQs and language abilities is relative to the amount parents speak to their children.

2. Children's academic successes at ages nine and ten are attributable to the amount of talk they hear from birth to age three.

3. Parents of advanced children talk significantly more to their children

than parents of children who are not as advanced.

The researchers culminated their work with the book Meaningful Differences in the Everyday Experience of Young American Children. In the book Hart and Risley wrote that "with few exceptions, the more parents talked to their children, the faster the children's vocabularies were growing and the higher the children's IQ test scores at age three and later." In addition, "The data revealed that the most important aspect of children's language experience is its amount." Finally, "differences in the amount of cumulative experience children had... were strongly linked to differences at age three in children's rates of vocabulary growth, vocabulary use, and general accomplishments and strongly linked to differences in school performance at age nine."[8]

What these researchers showed was that something so simple-the amount of words a child hears from a parent-has a profound effect on that child's academic success. (It should be noted that the researches demonstrated that it was not just a matter of hearing words, but, rather, spoken words from adults. Television, radio, and other electronic forms are not included in the cumulative count.)

The results of this study also found a troubling connection between family income and the amount of words a child hears. Hart and Risley explain that "National data shows that children in low-income households hear approximately 616 words per hour, nearly half as many words as heard by children in middle-income households (1,251) and less than one third as many words heard by children in high-income households (2,153). For a child's vocabulary to develop on an appropriate trajectory, children need to hear at least 21,000 words per day-the rough equivalent of reading Dr. Seuss's The Cat in the Hat nearly a dozen times a day."[9]

If you are reading this book while your child plays with an iPad you may want to reconsider your to do list for today. In other words, the 'hunch' a parent might have-that a child needs to have exposure to sophisticated technology and extensive language and mathematical interventions-may be completely flawed *based on science.*

Hart and Risley's research has been so widely accepted that an initiative called Providence Talks has been launched in Providence, Rhode Island via a $5 million dollar grant from Bloomberg Philanthropies. Rather using the money to give low income families an iPad, it is being used on small devices from the LENA Foundation that record the amount of words that a child hears throughout the course of a day. Filtering out electronic devices and noting environmental variances, researchers are able to work with parents to provide data that drives behavior changes and improvements. The devices could be described as a 'pedometer for speech.'

Hunch or science? Science. Simple or complicated? Simple. Easy or difficult to implement? Easy. Innovative? Yes.

Chapter 2

What's up with the title of this book?

"Everything that can be invented has been invented."

—*Charles H. Duell, Commissioner, U.S. Office of Patents, 1899.*

You may be asking at this point, 'so what's up with the title of this book, *Mustard Doesn't Go on Corn!* and what could mustard and corn possibly have to do with innovation?' On the surface, it may seem the answer is 'nothing.' However, as you will see, they have *everything* to do with innovation.

I once brought my young daughter to a small children's museum. Everywhere I looked I saw words like explore, discover, and imagine. In one section of the museum there was a small play kitchen that could accommodate about 10 kids. I was watching my daughter have a grand old time putting plastic grapes in the play oven when I saw a remarkable event. There was a little boy about 3 or 4 years old who had a plate with some plastic corn on it. He said to his mom, "OK, mom, I'm going to put mustard on your corn." Just as he was about to do so his mom said, in a semi-nurturing voice, "mustard doesn't go on corn." The kid's face dropped. What made it worse is what happened next. Another little kid very emphatically said, "No, mustard doesn't go on corn." You may be asking 'what's the big deal here?' But it was a big deal-to that child. And, it was at that moment in time I realized why innovation is often so difficult for companies and our society. Here was a little kid seeing words and images encouraging him to explore and be creative, and the second he does, boom –'mustard doesn't go on corn!' In a matter of seconds the kid had his idea shot down by an authority figure and was piled on by a peer. Sound familiar?

Being the instigator I am, I could not just sit back and watch this happen. I said, "I like mustard on corn." The kid looked confused. "I do. I put mustard on everything I eat." Still looking confused and a little hesitant he asked, "You do?" "Yup, even on spaghetti." Suddenly a slow rolling energy started to take over that little kitchen and within seconds other kids were getting involved. Suddenly mustard on corn didn't seem so foolish. "How about Cheerios?" someone asked. "Every day," I responded. And on and on it went, eventually with the other child who had originally dismissed such a 'foolish' idea joining in on the fun.

Let's play out this same scenario at work. A company has an 'innovation initiative' and puts up signs and banners with phrases like 'every idea counts' or 'innovation is king.' A person (the child who suggested putting mustard on corn) suggests an idea. The boss (the mother in the story above) publicly says 'that won't work.' A co-worker (the other child) then says, 'yeah that's not a good idea.' Now, imagine that a person like me was not there for support. *The idea dies.* Just like a seed thrown on a cement sidewalk, there is no chance of it growing. And, as described earlier, the answer to this issue is not contained in a PowerPoint slide from a weekend seminar at Harvard. It exists in the simple premise-and one that is supported by science and research-that it is simple behaviors coupled with a clear process to bring ideas to action that enables companies to become truly innovative, not pouring countless amounts of resources into glamorous posters, sophisticated presentations, and high priced advice-all of which are not needed. Just like the Twinkie or the designer shirt, you don't need a personal trainer with a PhD in nutrition to tell you fruit is better than Twinkies (wow that is tough to admit) or an MBA degree to calculate you don't have enough money for the shirt. In this workplace example, just as with the child at the museum, it is obvious-be open to ideas and respect the input of others. If your organization's culture does not promote an atmosphere of sincere respect and openness, how can you truly expect people to come forth with ideas? How can you have a workforce that is engaged and contributing more than simply doing their work? How can we focus on implementation of ideas when we don't even have ideas to implement?

In 1992, Psychology Today published an article titled *The Art of Creativity*. The authors stressed the importance of "Vanquishing negativity" to enable the creative process. They wrote "Apart from the structure of a company, the attitudes that pervade its operations can enhance or thwart creativity. One of the keys is building feelings of trust and respect to the point that people feel secure enough to express new ideas without fear of censure. This is because in the marketplace, imaginative thoughts have financial value. But an unimaginative, unreceptive attitude destroys opportunity. Someone who judges your imaginative thoughts, who refuses to listen to a new way of thinking or simply criticizes it, is a creativity killer of the first order. Cynicism and negativity are enemies of the creative spirit."(Goleman, Kaufman, Ray, 1992)[10] They go on to add that "But the degree of creativity is influenced by our feelings: our belief that we can speak without fear of retribution, our feeling of being trusted by others, a confidence in our own intuition. All affect how we respond to the information before us." Leigh Branham, in the book *The 7 Hidden Reasons Employees Leave* specifically mentions "being treated with disrespect" as one of the ways employees feel devalued and, ultimately drive their decision to leave a company.[11]

But what if you are not creative? Well, as of this moment, that notion is to be put to rest. EVERYONE is creative. *The Art of Creativity* article explains that "Our lives can be filled with creative moments, **whatever we do**, as long as we're flexible and open to new possibilities-willing to push beyond routine. The everyday expression of creativity often takes the form of trying out a new approach to a familiar dilemma. Yet half the world still thinks of creativity as a mysterious quality that the other half possesses. A good deal of research suggests, however, that **everyone is capable of tapping into his or her creative spirit.** We don't just mean getting better ideas: we're talking about a kind of general awareness that leads to greater enjoyment of your work and the people in your life:

23

a spirit that can improve collaboration and communication with others." (Goleman, Kaufman, Ray, 1992) [10]

Harvard Business School Professor, Teresa Amabile, a leading researcher in the study of creativity, supports the statements above by noting that "Everyone is capable of producing novel and useful ideas. Anyone can do some degree of creative work."[12] You-yes you-are creative and have something to offer.

Vanquishing negativity. Feelings of trust and respect. Speaking without fear of retribution. Open to new possibilities. Acknowledging that everyone is creative. *These* are the keys to innovation and building an innovative culture.

Chapter 3

Kids "get it"

"The greatest invention in the world is the mind of a child."

—Thomas Edison

But if everyone is creative, why do companies and organizations seem to continuously struggle to reach what many agree is necessary for a company to succeed and maybe even survive? Carl Sagan, the famous astronomer and scientist provides a succinct and poignant opinion. "Every kid starts out as a natural-born scientist, and then we beat it out of them. A few trickle through the system with their wonder and enthusiasm for science intact." (In the spirit of full disclosure, Sagan also astutely observed that "The fact that some geniuses were laughed at does not imply that all who are laughed at are geniuses. They laughed at Columbus, they laughed at Fulton, they laughed at the Wright brothers. But they also laughed at Bozo the Clown.") No child is born negative. No child, when offered candy and ice cream, says, "yeah but, the problem with that it is I might not eat my dinner." They take the ice cream and candy AND ask for whipped cream. We-as parents, as bosses, as the media, as peers, as fellow students-to use

Sagan's words, "beat it out of them." Then, years later, despite all the education, extracurricular activities, and focus on trying to help our children succeed, we continue to struggle to build innovative work environments. The irony of this is that we all were just fine until we went to one place-school.

Sir Ken Robinson, a leader in the field of education and known across the world for his books, and, most likely, his famous TED (Technology, Education, and Design) Talk titled, Do Schools Kills Creativity? Robinson, a brilliant author and witty and engaging speaker, tells the following story. "I heard [of] a little girl who was in a drawing lesson, she was 6 and she was at the back, drawing, and the teacher said this little girl hardly paid attention, and in this drawing lesson she did. The teacher was fascinated and she went over to her and she said, "What are you drawing?" and the girl said, "I'm drawing a picture of God." And the teacher said, "But nobody knows what God looks like." And the girl said, "They will in a minute."

Gordon MacKenzie, in the book *Orbiting the Giant Hairball: A Corporate Fool's Guide to Surviving with Grace*, talks about visiting elementary schools. "How many artists are there in the room? Would you please raise your hands? FIRST GRADE: En mass the children leapt from their seats, arms waving.

Every child was an artist. SECOND GRADE: About half the kids raised their hands, shoulder high, no higher. The hands were still. THIRD GRADE: At best, 10 kids out of 30 would raise a hand, tentatively, self-consciously. By the time I reached SIXTH GRADE, no more than one or two kids raised their hands, and then ever so slightly, betraying a fear of being identified by the group as a 'closet artist.' The point is: Every school I visited was participating in the suppression of creative genius."[13]

I had a friend of mine email me to say she was about to tell her daughter not to put ketchup on her green beans when she remembered the story I had told her about the children's museum, the mustard, and the corn. Rather than stop her daughter, she and her husband encouraged her. "My kids now eat their vegetables." First mustard and now ketchup. Is relish next? Innovation knows no bounds when it comes to condiments.

Imagine if she had suggested to her husband that they attend a week long workshop on innovation to develop unique ways for their children to eat vegetables. Even more ridiculous would be the notion of returning home after the workshop and delivering a PowerPoint presentation to their children.

Instead, she listened, enabled an idea to grow, and the results are in-her kids eat vegetables.

My wife and I have experienced this same phenomenon with our own children. Even before the age of ten, they 'got it' simply by my wife and 'modeling it.' The phrase "yeah but" is taboo in our house as is the notion of squashing other's ideas. Our children can often be heard saying "hey, no negativity" when a suggestion is dismissed or not met with respect and openness. And, it is critical to point out that they have the right and are actually encouraged to confront my wife and me when we head down the negative path. We, as the 'leaders,' are not off limits and must model, encourage, and foster an innovative environment.

I once had a participant in a workshop email me days later, telling me that he, as the coach of his daughter's basketball team, was feeling frustrated by the girls lack of engagement. He stopped practice, told them the mustard story, and did a few simple fun activities. Interestingly, he involved them more in the play calling and they won their next game. "One. Two. Three. Mustard Goes On Corn!" was the team's group celebration cheer. Again, the leader encourages involvement and engagement, ideas are listened to, and the results speak for themselves.

Let's go back to the workplace example. Imagine a couple of days later in a meeting the boss asks for more ideas. The person who had his idea slammed sits there quietly. He says nothing. Co-workers who saw his idea slammed also remain silent. What seemed to be a normal and innocuous event-the dismissal of an idea-will have wide reaching effects within the organization.

Chapter 4

Are we really just talking about engagement?

"There is no reason anyone would want a computer in their home."

—Ken Olson, president, chairman and founder of Digital Equipment Corp., 1977

What took place in the meeting with the boss and the employees in the previous chapter is an illustration of an aspect of what is known as Chaos Theory, and in this situation, the Butterfly Effect. "In chaos theory, the 'butterfly effect' is the sensitive dependence on initial conditions, where a small change at one place in a deterministic nonlinear system can result in large differences to a later state. The name of the effect, coined by Edward Lorenz, is derived from the theoretical example of a hurricane's formation being contingent on whether or not a distant butterfly had flapped its wings several weeks before." (Lorenz, 1963)[14]

Therefore, what on the surface was a fairly benign event-an idea being received without respect or openness-will, over time, result in massive disruption to the organization in terms of ideas being suppressed, employees not being actively engaged, and possibly an overall malaise within the culture of the company. Sound far-fetched? It's not.

The Gallup organization, a leader in data collection and analysis, recently reported that "Only 13% of employees worldwide are engaged at work, according to Gallup's new 142-country study on the *State of the Global Workplace.* In other words, about one in eight workers—roughly 180 million employees in the countries studied—are psychologically committed to their jobs and likely to be making positive contributions to their organizations." (Gallup, October 2013)[15] In addition, Gallup notes that "The bulk of employees worldwide—63%—are "not engaged," meaning they lack motivation and are less likely to invest discretionary effort in organizational goals or outcomes. And 24% are "actively disengaged," indicating they are unhappy and unproductive at work and liable to spread negativity to coworkers. In rough numbers, this translates into 900 million not engaged and 340 million actively disengaged workers around the globe."

While these statistics are global in nature, American and Canadian workers did fare better than their global counterparts with the highest percentage of engaged workers at 29 percent. 54 percent of American and Canadian workers are not engaged, and 18 percent are actively disengaged. (Gallup, October 2013). Therefore, US and Canadian workers are tops-with over 70% of workers either not engaged or actively disengaged. Gallup summarizes its' finding by noting that "Regardless of region or industry, businesses seeking to adapt to rapidly changing global economic conditions must learn how to maintain high-productivity workplaces and grow their customer bases in widely varying social, cultural, and economic environments. Systems for reliably measuring and improving employee engagement across industries and regions worldwide are vital to that goal. Business leaders worldwide must raise the bar on employee engagement. Increasing workplace engagement is vital to achieving sustainable growth for companies, communities, *and* countries-and for putting the global economy back on track to a more prosperous and peaceful future."

Would you start or invest in a company where, statistically speaking, you knew that over 70% of the workers were either not engaged or actively disengaged? Walk down the hallway and count the first ten people you see. Again, statistically speaking, only three are actively engaged and seven are either not engaged or actively disengaged. Based on Gallup's research two of the ten people are "unhappy and unproductive at work and [are] liable to spread negativity to coworkers."

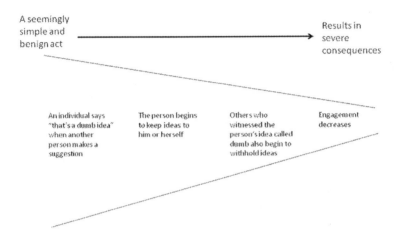

Figure1: Butterfly Effect and negative responses to ideas

Is this an exaggeration? Let's think back to the mustard story. There were about ten people in that play kitchen at the children's museum and it took only took two (the parent and the other young child) to, in effect, destroy the engagement of all the other children. The statistics don't lie and Chaos Theory and the Butterfly Effect and not the things of fanciful imaginations. They have been studied extensively and are proven phenomenon.

But wait. If one 'yeah but' or the squashing of an idea can have such a negative ripple effect, what about positive phrases like 'yes and' or 'that's interesting, tell me more'-can they leverage the Butterfly Effect in the opposite manner and set of a cascading explosion of positive effects on an organization? The answer is yes. The Butterfly Effect does not only cause earthquakes or floods. It can also produce positive benefits and beneficial outcomes as well.

The Society for Human Resource Management Employee notes that "engagement is strongly influenced by organizational characteristics, such as a reputation for integrity, good internal communication and a culture of innovation." (SHRM, 2007)[16] Therefore, if a company or organization is able to create a culture of innovation-specifically one built on a foundation of respect and openness-then employee engagement will increase.

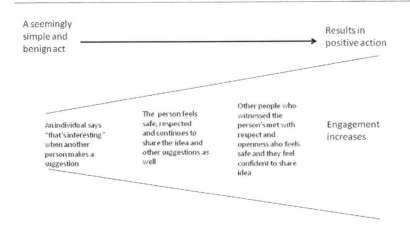

Figure2: Butterfly Effect and positive responses to ideas

Creating an innovative culture will help an organization generate and implement ideas that help overcome obstacles and exceed market expectations. It will also enable a company to lower employee turn-over, be more productive, and increase employee engagement. In a nut shell-"it" will dramatically improve an organization's bottom line-especially since everything that a company needs to do to create an innovative culture is essentially free and immediately and readily available in every employee.

Before we move to the next chapter take a moment to reflect on what you have read and, more importantly, and assign some dollar values to the items below.

Item	Dollar value (cost)
Not being open to ideas	
Cost to replace an employee	
Cost of low engagement	
Cost of missed opportunities due to employees not being willing to share ideas	
Cost of listening to ideas, being open to suggestions, and having respect for everyone's input	FREE

Still not convinced? There's more.

Chapter 5

Everyone has a role to play

"Computers in the future may weigh no more than 1.5 tons."

—Popular Mechanics, forecasting the relentless march of science, 1949

Hopefully you have come to appreciate that innovation is not something that can simply be left to 'those creative folks'. Building an innovative culture must involve everyone from top to bottom. For example, a company can't proclaim to have a culture of integrity and then say 'but these folks over here get to lie or do some unethical stuff every once in a while'. That would be ludicrous. The same is true for innovation. If innovation is what an organization truly wants then there needs to be a commitment from everyone at all levels to say this is something we value and we will live and demonstrate every day. With that said, there is no harm starting at a team or group level provided that the entire team or group is completely on board. I have worked with countless companies where various groups or departments from a wide range of industries and functional areas who have expressed an interest in creating an innovative culture and have done so with great success. The key was that all members of the team were involved in the process.

Corporate culture is pervasive and powerful as it either encourages or hampers change in the organization. For employees, corporate culture is either the glue that binds employees to the organization or the wind that blows them away.[17]

The term organization includes corporations, non-profits, schools-anywhere a collective group is working together. Organization can even include sports teams.

Examples-The Detroit Pistons and the Los Angeles Dodgers

Just like having to admit eating Twinkies are bad for you, writing about the Detroit Pistons is painful. As a lifelong Boston Celtics fan (or fanatic according to my wife), it is tough to acknowledge that the Pistons teams of the 1980's-the ones who beat the Celtics-have something extraordinary to add to the discussion on innovation.

Like me, author and ESPN analyst, Bill Simmons, is a huge Boston sports fan. In 2009 Simmons wrote The Book of Basketball which is a very entertaining and well researched history of the National Basketball Association (NBA) and the American Basketball Association (ABA). While Simmons set out to document the history of the NBA, along the way he made a significant contribution to the conversation around corporate culture.

Isiah Thomas, former Detroit Piston and NBA hall-of-famer, shared this insight with Simmons. "The secret of basketball is that it's not about basketball."[18] Thomas goes onto explain that it is about team chemistry or, in context for our discussion-culture. Simmons adds that "Fans overlook The Secret completely. Nobody writes about The Secret because of a general lack of sophistication about basketball; even the latest 'revolution' of basketball statistics

47

centers more around evaluating players against one another over capturing their effect on a team. The fans don't get it. Actually, it goes deeper than that—I'm not sure who gets it. We measure players by numbers, only the playoffs roll around and teams that play together, kill themselves defensively, sacrifice personal success and ignore statistics invariably win the title. We have trouble processing the 'teamwork over talent' thing. But how do you keep stats for 'best chemistry' and 'most unselfish' or even 'most tangible and consistent effect on a group of teammates'? It's impossible. That's why we struggle to comprehend professional basketball."

I would expand on Simmons' statement to include innovation, i.e. "That's why we struggle to comprehend *innovation*." What Thomas was explaining and Simmons was writing was that it is the culture that is the key. Innovation is not about one person (a superstar, if you will, to keep with the sports analogy) coming up with a great idea and single handedly winning the game. It is about people buying into a vision and philosophy.

The sports world is littered with examples of when 'the best team didn't win' or, 'when a superstar didn't carry a team to a championship.'

In 1988, one of the most memorable events in baseball history took place. Kirk Gibson, a star for the Los Angeles Dodgers, was sidelined with a knee injury and was considered doubtful for the World Series. In a moment straight out of the movie *The Natural* with Robert Redford, Gibson hit a homerun in the bottom of the ninth inning versus the Oakland A's to win the game. While the image of Gibson fist pumping as he hobbled around the bases is what is remembered most, it is the innovative idea and that took place *before* his at bat that deserves more credit. ESPN.com recounts what happened.[19]

Down to one out in the ninth inning, Dodgers manager Tommy Lasorda has Mike Davis pinch hit for Alfredo Griffin. Interestingly, Davis was only hitting .196 for the year. But the goal was not to get a hit-it was to disrupt A's star pitcher, Dennis Eckersley. In addition, Lasorda sends out a decoy to the on-deck circle, David Anderson, knowing that if Davis can get on base, he will be able to give Gibson, who is now in the locker room stretching and warming up, a chance to hit. Gibson was in so much pain he could barely walk.

In and out of the batter's box goes Davis, enough to frustrate Eckersley and draw a walk. ""*A two-out walk* to any hitter is inexcusable, and I don't do it very often. I tried to go right at him, but everything sailed outside. He was stepping in and out of the box a lot, disrupting my rhythm," Eckersley would say later. Gibson comes up, hits a homerun, and the rest is history.

Therefore, while it was Gibson-the superstar-hit the homerun, it was an innovative idea-disrupting the pitcher enough just to get someone on base-that led to the dramatics. What took place in those few moments in Los Angeles did not magically happen. It was the result of having the right culture in place, one where an idea as *simple* as stepping in and out of the batter's box to draw a walk could be suggested and, more importantly, acted on by a role player that listened and executed the idea perfectly. I can think of many teams and players for which this never would have happened due to ego. But the Dodgers 'got it.' The goal was not to hit a home run, it was to win the game.

And, again, the idea was *simple*.

I have a concern with some of the innovation courses or training that is done with companies and organizations. While there are fantastic and brilliant people at some of the top firms and universities doing great work in this field, the idea that a few select executives can travel to Cambridge, Massachusetts, return a week later, and be able to build an innovative culture across an organization is questionable. In addition the notion that a team of consultants can parachute in, build sustainable change, and then eject out is one that creates skepticism-and a large fee for professional services. If these approaches worked so well then the courses and development programs would have ceased to exist years ago based on the large numbers of people to have attended such workshops and have returned to their job enlightened. Also, the wisdom imparted by consultants would have been captured, disseminated, and implemented across all companies and organizations across the world and there would be no need for this book. But there is.

Chapter 6

Creating a POP! Culture®
crazy vs. normal

The opposite of creativity is cynicism.

—Esa Saarinen

Please allow me to stress again that I do think there is great work being done around innovation, and, in particular, design based thinking. Companies such as Innosight and IDEO have great approaches as do universities such as Stanford and the Massachusetts Institute of Technology. However, these courses and services can often be very expensive (a three day innovation course at MIT is over $2500 per person plus travel and living expenses) and are not what I will describe as easily scalable to all members of an organization (when is the last time a front line assembly worker attended one of these classes off site at a prominent university?) Stanford has a free online offering from its Design School called *Design Thinking Action Lab*. They, along with other universities like Penn State are offering other classes and learning opportunities for free that cover topics of commercialization, creativity, and business models. However, I am convinced, based on the science, research, and years of seeing firsthand how quickly the approach in this book can transform a team, group, or company, that unless the approach is simple and easily accessible to EVERYONE in a company, the goal of building a truly innovative organization will not be achieved. What I propose is that the process and philosophy in this book be used to complement other innovation efforts. For example, Stanford's design based thinking is proven to work. However, if people are not open to new ideas and respectful to other points of view, the foundation will not have been set and the effort will not reach its full potential.

Example-The Checklist

Tour any hospital in America and you will see sophisticated diagnostic imaging machines, computers running advanced software applications, and medicines developed by countless years of research and scientific exploration. However, based on statistics, it is a wonder that anyone wants to be treated in a hospital in the United States.

Atul Gawande, a surgeon at Brigham and Women's Hospital in Boston, Massachusetts and an Associate Professor of Medicine at Harvard Medical School published a book in 2009 named The Checklist Manifesto.[20] In the book he shares some alarming statistics with respect to hospital visits and, more specifically, line infections in the Intensive Care Unit. He writes that "at any point, we are as apt to harm as we are to heal. Line infections are so common that they are considered a routine complication. ICUs put five million lines into patients each year, and national statistics show that after ten days 4 percent of those lines become infected. Line infections occur in eighty thousand people a year in the United States and are fatal between 5 and 28 percent of the time, depending on how sick one is at the start. Those who survive line infections spend on average a week longer in intensive care. And this is just one of many risks. After ten days with a urinary catheter, 4 percent of American ICU patients develop a bladder infection. After ten days on a ventilator, 6 percent develop bacterial pneumonia, resulting in death 40 to 45 percent of the time. All in all, about half of ICU patients end up experiencing a serious complication, and once that occurs the chances of survival drop sharply."

And this issue is not limited to the Unites States. Gawande goes onto add that across the world "The volume of surgery had grown so swiftly that, without anyone's quite realizing, it has come to exceed global totals for childbirth— only with a death rate ten to one hundred times higher. Although most of the time a given procedure goes just fine, often it doesn't: estimates of complication rates for hospital surgery range from 3 to 17 percent. While incisions have gotten smaller and recoveries have gotten quicker, the risks remain serious. Worldwide, at least seven million people a year are left disabled and at least one million dead—a level of harm that approaches that of malaria, tuberculosis, and other traditional public health concerns."

So where does one start when trying to tackle such an enormous healthcare problem? Gawande started with airplanes and skyscrapers. He ended up with a simple solution-one that involves using simple checklists and creating a culture of respect, openness, and teamwork.

"Take the safe surgery checklist. If someone discovered a new drug that could cut down surgical complications with anything remotely like the effectiveness of the checklist, we would have television ads with minor celebrities extolling its virtues. Detail men would offer free lunches to get doctors to make it part of their practice. Government programs would research it. Competitors would jump in to make newer and better versions. If the checklist were a medical device, we would have surgeons clamoring for it, lining up at display booths at surgical conferences to give it a try, hounding their hospital administrators to get one for them—because, damn it, doesn't providing good care matter to those pencil pushers?

That's what happened when surgical robots came out—drool-inducing twenty-second-century $1.7 million remote-controlled machines designed to help surgeons do laparoscopic surgery with more maneuverability inside patients' bodies and fewer complications. The robots increased surgical costs massively and have so far improved results only modestly for a few operations, compared with standard laparoscopy. Nonetheless, hospitals in the United States and abroad have spent billions of dollars on them."

Gawande writes that the results of his initial research with eight hospitals across the world showed that "the rate of major complications for surgical patients in all eight hospitals fell by 36 percent after introduction of the checklist. Deaths fell 47 percent. The results had far outstripped what we'd dared to hope for, and all were statistically highly significant. Infections fell by almost half. The number of patients having to return to the operating room after their original operations because of bleeding or other technical problems fell by one-fourth. Overall, in this group of nearly 4,000 patients, 435 would have been expected to develop serious complications based on our earlier observation data. But instead just 277 did. Using the checklist had spared more than 150 people from harm — and 27 of them from death."

So everyone and every hospital is on-board, correct? How could doctors, nurses, and administrators not want something so simple and powerful implemented? It should be case closed, right? Wrong. When his team surveyed the doctors who used the checklist, "There was about 80 percent who thought that this was something they wanted to continue to use. But 20 percent remained strongly against it. They said, 'This is a waste of my time, I don't think it makes any difference.' And then we asked them, 'If you were to have an operation, would you want the checklist?' Ninety-four percent wanted the checklist."[21]

Gawande points out that "Just ticking boxes is not the ultimate goal here. Embracing a culture of teamwork and discipline is." Again, the culture is the key. He discusses at length the importance of teamwork, communication, and respect. And, just like the premise of innovation, dramatic changes in healthcare are, in fact, easy.

Here are a few interesting reactions from readers of Gawande's work:

2 stars-I kept thinking there was going to be this profound moment in the book when the big idea bursts into view and wows me with how it has solved so many things and can change the world...then I realized it's a book about checklists. Isn't it kind of obvious that they work?

2 stars-It's like reading Gladwell, but instead of a catchy Big Idea this book just advocates for making lists.

2 stars-Except for the exciting medical cases the book cites, the core concept is a no-brainer really. We all have heard it before and most of us would know checklists work.

Why the negativity?

_____

The *Mustard Approach*, for lack of a better phrase, is a process that is fast, efficient, and is centered on what I call the creation of a POP! Culture® where POP stands for the Positive Outlook Principle. A POP! Culture is one based in respect and openness and utilizes a simple process to move ideas from thoughts to *action*. (I can't stress enough the word action for without action, ideas are just, well, ideas.) A POP! Culture is one where *every employee* is constantly sharing and implementing new ideas.

Normal	POP! Culture®
Negative (Balloon Effect)	Positive (High Five)
Process for innovation complicated or none at all	Process for innovation simple

Rewards, incentives, large amount of costly resources devoted to innovation	Innovation is FREE and readily available
Employee engagement average or low	Employee engagement above average or high
"Yeah but..."	"Yes, and..."
"The problem with that is..."	"Help me understand..."
"That won't happen"	"How do we make that happen?"
Ideas often immediately dismissed	Ideas met with openness and respect
Leave things to the 'creative few'	Everyone is creative
People hesitant to share ideas	Everyone constantly sharing and implementing new ideas
Ideas judged and debated the split second they are shared	Ideas judged and evaluated after respectful and rigorous consideration
Talking and sharing of ideas is key	Listening to shared ideas is key
No or complicated process for innovation	Simple process for innovation
Too many ideas are a distraction	The more ideas the better; we have a process to prioritize them

Figure 3. A POP! Culture

Just how important is culture when it comes to innovation? After studying innovation among 759 companies based in 17 major markets, researchers Gerard J. Tellis, Jaideep C.

Prabhu and Rajesh K. Chandy found that corporate culture was a much more important driver of radical innovation than labor, capital, government or national culture.[22] In 2013 MIT's *Sloan Management Review* published an article titled *How Innovative is Your Company's Culture?* The authors listed key components to building an innovative culture, two of which were values and climate. With respect to values, they note that *"Values* drive priorities and decisions, which are reflected in how a company spends its time and money. Truly innovative enterprises spend generously on being entrepreneurial, promoting creativity and encouraging continuous learning. The values of a company are less what the leaders say or what they write in the annual reports than what they do and invest in. Values manifest themselves in how people behave and spend, more than in how they speak."[23] In terms of climate, they write that *"Climate* is the tenor of workplace life. An innovative climate cultivates engagement and enthusiasm, challenges people to take risks within a safe environment, fosters learning and encourages independent thinking.[24]

In my workshops there are two exercises that I take participants through to help begin to see and experience the power of a POP! Culture. The first is what I call the High-Five. Participants are asked to stand, raise their right or left hand (I had to add 'or left' because some people were concerned they were taking an oath of some type) and then walk around the room, high five as many people as possible, and, when they do, yell-yes yell-the word "yes!" This usually gets people up and moving and brings some energy and laughter to the room. Once people are seated again, I give them an assignment-to high five a complete stranger outside of work, preferably at a train station, a coffee stop, i.e. somewhere public and where people are not expecting this type of behavior. The response is predictable. "They will think we are crazy" "They will ask what is wrong with you." "I will get punched or hurt." (This last response seems more prevalent in the Northeast).

But wait, I ask. You are energetic, smiling, and enthusiastic and people will think you are crazy. Interesting.

I then do a second exercise that I call The Balloon Effect.™ This exercise is the opposite of High Five. Participants pair up and one person has a balloon. I ask the person to blow up the balloon and explain that this represents the sharing of an idea. It takes energy. It is visible. The person is, in effect, exposed. I then ask the second person to take a paperclip and open it, forming a pin. The room knows what is coming.

The second person is going to pop the balloon. However, I provide very explicit instructions-the person must look at the person holding the balloon directly in the eyes, laugh at the person, say 'that is a bad idea,' and then pop the balloon. Pop. Pop. Pop. Balloon (idea) after balloon (idea) is shattered in a fraction of a second. Again, there is laughter and people have fun with it. What happens next is telling.

I ask the participants how many people have ever had something like this happen to them at work. Every hand goes up. I ask people if they have ever popped someone's idea. Every hand goes up. I ask them what they would think of doing this exercise over and over for the next thirty minutes. People shake their heads 'no.' We then have a discussion around what if someone was new to this company and saw an idea get publicly dismissed in such a disrespectful manner. Would they be enthusiastic to share ideas? The answer, again, is 'no.' I ask one final question-would you consider this normal behavior? The answer is *'yes.'*

A high five to a stranger is crazy yet reacting publicly to another person's idea with negativity and disrespect is normal? How can this be? How can companies and organizations possibly become innovative if these are the norms from which we are operating? The answer is obvious-they can't. Unless what organizations consider *crazy* becomes normal, and what we consider *normal* becomes crazy organizations, companies, teams, groups-even families and schools-will be not become innovative environments that welcome ideas with respect and openness.

Am I saying that a high five is the solution to creating an innovative culture? No. However, juxtapose these activities (and there are many more that will be explored in detail) with complicated PowerPoint slides or graphs with intricate details. Which do you think employee can grasp more easily? This is why the *Mustard Approach* works.

A POP! Culture, like other topics discussed thus far, is not something developed on gut feel. It is also not simply a rah-rah let's get people pumped up endeavor. It is a process for which science and research supports the methodology.

Chapter 7

Science weighs in

"Discovery consists of looking at the same thing as everyone else and thinking something different."

—*Albert Szent Gyorgi*

Marcial Losada, a researcher at MIT and the University of Michigan, published a paper titled *The Complex Dynamics of High Performance Teams*. He shares that "From a qualitative perspective, my own assessments of these teams can be summarized as follows: high performance teams were characterized by an atmosphere of buoyancy that lasted during the whole meeting. By showing appreciation and encouragement to other members in the team, they created emotional spaces that were expansive and opened possibilities for action and creativity. They were also fun to watch and there was rarely a dull moment during their meetings. In addition, they accomplished their tasks with ease and grace. In stark contrast, low performance teams struggled with their tasks, operated in very restrictive emotional spaces created by lack of mutual support and enthusiasm, often in an atmosphere charged with distrust and cynicism. The medium performance teams operated in emotional spaces that were not as restrictive as the low performance teams, but not nearly as expansive as the high performance teams. They were able to finish their tasks as planned, but not with the novelty and creativity characteristic of high performance teams."[25] He adds "I will call "emotional space" the ratio of positivity to negativity; high ratios imply expansive emotional spaces and low ratios restrictive emotional spaces. High performance teams should be able to create expansive emotional spaces; consequently, the positivity-negativity ratio should be high and we would expect this dimension to be unbalanced towards positivity."

Stepping aside from the workplace for a moment, Losada also shares that "that unless couples are able to maintain a high ratio of positivity to negativity, it is highly likely that the relationship will end."[26] The next time your spouse or significant other suggests something you may want to hold off on that 'yeah but' or 'the problem with that is' as a first reaction to his or her idea.

What is interesting about Losada's work is that he leverages the efforts of Lorenz-the originator of Chaos Theory described in chapter 1. Although his approach has been considered controversial by some, Losada writes that "Overall and in agreement with expectations, high performance teams had expansive emotional spaces, and, most importantly, all the trajectories in phase space showed chaotic dynamics, like Kauffman had observed in his networks. These chaotic dynamics indicate that the type of balance reached by high performance teams, in terms of inquiry-advocacy and other-self orientation, is the product of a sophisticated pattern of interaction, typical of nonlinear systems, where the unpredictability of the trajectories creates the topology necessary for the creativity and novelty observed in highly productive teams."

If that didn't get your head spinning, let's add that B.V. Chirikov, a physicist at the Institute of Nuclear Physics in Novosibirsk, shares that there is an "inexhaustible diversity and richness of dynamical chaos. It presents... the surprising complexity of the structures and evolution characteristic of a broad range of processes in nature, including the highest, levels of its organization. *Moreover, dynamical chaos is a necessary part of creative activity.*"[27]

Wow. That was a lot to take in. Four words: positivity good, negativity bad.

Positive Organizational Behavior is the study and application of positively oriented human resource strengths and psychological capacities that can be measured, developed, and effectively managed for performance improvement in today's workplace.[28] A major component of Positive Organizational Behavior is the confidence level of an individual. As Luthans writes, "rich theory and considerable research support clearly indicates that the more confident the individual, the more likely the choice will be made to really get into the task and welcome the challenge; the more effort and motivation will be given to successfully accomplish the task; and the more persistence there will be when obstacles are encountered or even when there is initial failure."[29] In addition to confidence, resiliency also plays a prominent role in Positive Organizational Behavior. "Resiliency is the capability of individuals to cope successfully in the face of significant change, adversity, or risk. This capability changes over time and is enhanced by protective factors in the individual and environment."[30]

Luthans adds that "Led by Seligman and a core group of other well-known research-oriented positive psychologists such as Ed Diener (2000), Christopher Peterson (2000), and Rick Snyder (2000), the aim of positive psychology is to shift the emphasis away from what is wrong with people to what is right with people-to focus on strengths (as opposed to weaknesses), to be interested in resilience (as opposed to vulnerability), and to be concerned with enhancing and developing wellness, prosperity and the good life (as opposed to the remediation of pathology). Unlike the popular 'feel good' positive approaches of the past, such as Norman Vincent Peale's famous message of the 'power of positive thinking,' or the recent best-sellers by Covey and Spencer Johnson, positive psychology follows its heritage of insisting on sound theory and research before moving on to application and practice."

In a POP! Culture the focus is on what Luthan's describes-focus on the positive versus the negative or, as I have described, put effort into how to make things happen versus why they can't happen. Also like the research cited above, a POP! Culture is not to be confused with 'feel good approaches' or 'motivational speakers.' It is a both a mindset and a methodology that enables organizations to bring out the best in all employees, generate new ideas, and act on and implement innovations that produce results for the enterprise.

Example: The Apple Store

One Sunday morning I went to a local mall to get questions answered regarding one of my Apple devices. Whether it was my iMac, iPod, iPad, iPhone, I can't remember. What I do remember, however, is walking into the mall about 11:50 am and seeing a completely desolate shopping center except for one area-the space outside the Apple Store. Not only were there people, there was a line. A long line. There was not a new product being introduced or a sale. It was just the normal busyness that Apple Stores around the world manage every day.

In May of 2001, Apple opened its first retail store at the Tyson's Corner Galleria just outside of Washington, DC. That same month Businessweek published an article titled, *Sorry Steve: Here's Why Apple Stores Won't Work* which included the following. In the article the author complete pans the idea of the Apple Store, citing reasons including hard core financial data and projects. He goes so far as to write, ""*I give them two years before they're turning out the lights on a very painful and expensive mistake. Maybe its time for Steve Jobs to stop thinking so differently."*[31]

In 2011, Gigaom.com wrote that "Ten years later, there are 324 Apple Stores: 233 in the U.S., and 91 international locations. In terms of foot traffic, Apple saw its billionth retail visitor last month, with 71 million in the last quarter alone, up 51 percent year over year. The increasing number of visitors can be ascribed not only to the popularity of Apple products, but location of stores. In the U.S., the goal has always been to have 85 percent of the population within driving distance of an Apple Store, which has often meaning paying a premium for retail space. Bu it's been a strategy that's paid off."[32]

We can debate whether Steve Jobs was too much of a perfectionist or too difficult to work for. However, what is indisputable is the importance he placed on Apple's values and company culture. As Fast Company wrote in

2011, "These core values are the reason that Apple products have been so consistently excellent, and they are the reason that you can walk into any Apple store across the country and have essentially the same experience. From sales associates to top executives, Apple is united by a common culture. And it is that culture that ensures that Apple customers enjoy the experience that they have come to expect whenever they interact with Apple—whether that means using their iPhone, visiting an Apple store, or calling Apple's technical support line."[33]

The Apple store is one of the best examples of how negativity could have crushed a company. Imagine if the 'yeah but' or 'the problem with the store concept is' camps had won out. But they didn't and Apple was number 6 on the Fortune 500 at the time of this writing. In 2001 they were 236.

On an aside, Jobs was known to wear Levi's jeans which is a little ironic since the person who helped launch the Apple Store was the CEO of The Gap. What this has to do with innovation I don't know but now you can sound smart and witty and your next party.

We know we want positive over negative. We know we want to have a POP! Culture. What we need now is a plan. Here it is.

Chapter 8

The fog of negativity

"Once our minds are 'tattooed' with negative thinking, our chances for long-term success diminish"

—*John Maxwell*

The first step in creating a POP! Culture is to do a 'reboot' of the system of sorts. Since we are, in a sense, wiping out countless years of negative conditioning, the process for this 'reboot' of our internal thought processes needs to very simple, thus the concept that innovation is EASY. No one is born negative based on the research and science explaining that everyone is creative. However, based on general life experiences-school, the media, etc.-phrases like 'yeah but' and 'the problem with that it is' have become normal and even *expected*. Here is an example.

I have a friend who is a lawyer and loves to argue. In fact, he gets paid to argue-it is his job. Say left, and he says right. Say up, he says down. Say go, he says stop. While he is the exact type of person you would want to have represent you in a court room, it is often painful to have a discussion with him-*about anything*. Once, while driving to his home, I was listening to the radio. The radio host indicated that there was some breaking news that John Roberts was going to be named as the Chief Justice of the United States Supreme Court. Thinking my friend, as an attorney, would be interested in this news, I shared it with him when I arrived at his house. The conversation went something like this:

My friend:	"No way," he said.
Me:	"What do you mean 'no way?'"
My friend:	"He has only been on the bench a short time. He is too new. He doesn't have the experience. That's not going to happen."
Me:	"This isn't my opinion. I just heard it on the radio on the ride down."
My friend:	"Yeah but it is Saturday."
Me:	"What?"
My friend:	"It's not even a weekday. How can this be accurate?"
Me:	"I don't even know what that means."
My friend:	"Do you really think Bush [the President at the time] would nominate him?"

Me: "I have no idea. I am just telling you what I heard on the news. I didn't go to law school."

My friend: "No way. Not going to happen."

Imagine sound of me banging head against wall out of frustration. I was not offering an opinion or making a suggestion. I was sharing what a major news source was reporting as *fact*.

In defense of my friend, I am convinced that he is so conditioned to fight and argue that he doesn't even realize how frustrating a conversation like this can become. And *that* is this issue. There are probably many people reading this book who have, during the first two chapters, have had more than a few 'yeah buts' creep into their thoughts.

The first step is not to eliminate the negativity, but simply build awareness of just how negative we can be and the damage this can cause to the innovative process. Let's take a look at media for a moment, and, more specifically, cable news programming. On October 15, 2004, Jon Stewart, former host of Comedy Central's The Daily Show, was a guest on CNN's *Crossfire*, at the time hosted by Republican Tucker Carlson and Democrat Paul Begala. The episode, which became very contentious and argumentative, starts by Jon Stewart asking one basic question, "why do we have to fight?" He goes onto add, "It's hurting America. But I wanted to come here today and say stop, stop, stop, stop hurting America.[34] Carlson and Begala, expecting more of a comedy routine, started to push back on Stewart trying to defend that they were a debate show. "No, no, no, no, that would be great. To do a debate would be great," said Steward. "But that's like saying pro wrestling is a show about athletic competition."

Stewart raises a great point. While he welcomes a debate (a constructive dialogue where opposing points of view are discussed) he is not advocating fighting or confrontational behaviors. Putting this into the context of innovation, thorough debate of an idea is welcomed, especially as the suggestion moves toward implementation and the allocation of resources. What we don't need is an idea being blasted the instant it is presented. To echo Stewart, "why do we have to fight?"

Building on the example of the CNN show *Crossfire*, let's examine what could be described as the most dysfunctional team currently on the planet-the United States Congress-and the overall political process and discourse in the country. At the time of this writing American's approval rating of Congress was at 13%, up from an all-time low of 9% in 2013.[35] It is also important to note that Congress has not had an approval rating above 20% in the last three years. Congress became so ineffective in 2011 that it helped lead to the credit agency, Standard & Poor, downgrading the credit rating for America citing dysfunctional policymaking in Washington as a factor in the downgrade. "The political brinksmanship of recent months highlights what we see as America's governance and policymaking becoming less stable, less effective, and less predictable than what we previously believed." (Standard & Poor, 2011)

The reaction was predictable. Instead of taking the message to heart and using it as a rallying cry to set partisan politics aside and get to work, it became a contest of 'who's to blame.' Republicans blaming Democrats. Democrats blaming Republicans. Tea Party members blaming everyone. TV and radio 'pundits' arguing and yelling. And on and on it went. Rather than working together and sincerely trying to address a major crisis facing the nation, the dysfunction became even worse. I am convinced that the reason for so many of America's ills lies in the inability for politicians and even average citizens to sincerely listen to each other, be open to ideas, and be constructive versus destructive when tackling major issues. I fail to recognize how a talk show host who does nothing but criticize others and drives a divisive wedge between groups is helpful in terms of getting things done.

In 2014 this sentiment was echoed by billionaire entrepreneur and philanthropist, Michael Bloomberg. Speaking at Harvard's 2014 Commencement, Bloomberg shared the observation that major issues facing the nation are not decided by engaging with one another "but by trying to shout each other down."

Here is a challenge for you. Pick something you are passionate about-politics, sports, religion-and have a conversation with someone who you know has a different opinion on the subject than you do. Rather than try to tell them why you are right, why they are wrong, and why they should change their point of view (which is not going to happen, by the way), sincerely try to learn about their positions through respectful questions and listening. What was the result? What did you learn about yourself?

I once had a mentor who shared with me one of the most valuable lessons I have ever received. In a cab ride to a client location he and I were talking and he asked me "Rich, what do you think the role of a mediator is?" He was not using the pure definition of the role or referring to a specific situation. I said the trite 'help people agree' and 'come up with a solution' etc. "No," he said. "It is to create doubt." Puzzled, I asked him to elaborate. "When doubt is created in peoples' minds, they realize their ideas are not absolute and perfect. They become open to suggestions, and eventually move off their entrenched positions." Amazingly brilliant. I have yet to meet a person who is 100% right yet have met many, many individuals who will tell you they are. Imagine if for a moment, the members of the US Congress acknowledged that they are not perfect and that everyone brings value to the conversation. Then, imagine they had respect and openness for others' ideas, and possessed a sincere willingness to work together, and, dare I say, explore innovative solutions to the matters at hand. Would the United States be in the financial situation it finds itself? Would we be describing the country as 'blue states' and 'red states?' It was Abraham Lincoln who said "A house divided against itself cannot stand." He was right in 1858 and he would be right today. Politics in America needs to embrace the concept of a POP! Culture-respect, openness, and a simple process to move ideas to action.

Bestselling author, consultant, businessman, and organizational and family expert, Stephen Covey, sold over 15 million copies of his book 7 Habits of Highly Effective People.[36] Habit 5, *Seek first to understand then to be understood*, is precisely what is needed for constructive dialogue AND for innovation to flourish. He writes:

> *"Communication is the most important skill in life. We spend most of our waking hours communicating. But consider this: You've spent years learning how to read and write, years learning how to speak. But what about listening? What training or education have you had that enables you to listen so that you really, deeply understand another human being from that individual's own frame of reference? Comparatively few people have had any training in listening at all. And, for the most part, their training has been in the personality ethic of technique, truncated from the character base and the relationship base absolutely vital to authentic understanding of another person." He adds that ""Seek first to understand" involves a very deep*

shift in paradigm. We typically seek first to be understood. Most people do not listen with the intent to understand; they listen with the intent to reply. They're either speaking or preparing to speak. They're filtering everything through their own paradigms, reading their autobiography into other people's lives."

Covey's book is not the 87 Effective habits or the 1,021 Effective Habits. It is THE SEVEN Effective habits. Communication, and more importantly, listening, is so important that it made the final cut of the most important things that highly effective people do.

Are you an empathetic listener as defined by Covey above? Or, like most people, including myself, when you are 'listening' are you preparing what you want to say or how you want to respond? Think back to the last time you were presented with an idea. Did you say 'yeah but' or, instead, reply with something like 'that sounds interesting...can you help me understand.' This is CRITICAL and ESSENTIAL to innovation because it is impossible to build on-or even judge an idea-without fully understanding it. In addition, when a person shares and idea and he or she is given the opportunity to explain his or her thoughts in more detail, you are expressing respect and openness, which, in turn, leads to more engaged employees. Finally, think back to another idea that you implemented. Did what you implemented look exactly like what you started with or did it change and morph into something else as you worked through a process over time? Most likely, it what you acted on was not carried out verbatim as expressed in the initial thought. Innovation and creativity are like a famous skit from Saturday Night Live in 1976 where John Belushi explains how March comes in like a lion and goes out like a lamb. However, in the skit, the lion takes on many forms and twists along the way, especially in different countries like *"Norway, March comes in like a polar bear and goes out like a walrus"* or *"the case of Honduras where March comes in like a lamb and goes out like a salt marsh harvest mouse."*[37]

> *John Belushi: Thank you Chevy. Well, another winter is almost over and March true to form has come in like a lion, and hopefully will go out like a lamb. At least that's how March works here in the United States. But did you know that March behaves differently in other countries? In Norway, for example, March comes in like a*

polar bear and goes out like a walrus. Or, take the case of Honduras where March comes in like a lamb and goes out like a salt marsh harvest mouse.

Let's compare this to the Maldive Islands where March comes in like a wildebeest and goes out like an ant. A tiny, little ant about this big. [holds thumb and index fingers a small distance apart] Unlike the Malay Peninsula where March comes in like a worm-eating fernbird and goes out like a worm-eating fernbird. In fact, their whole year is like a worm-eating fernbird.

The same is true for ideas. Sometimes what comes in as an idea to build a computer.... comes out as an iPad. Bada Bing! That is a punch line. My point is that Apple Computer is now just Apple. What started out as a computer company has become so much more. Watches. Tablets. TV. Music.

There are countless other shows on Foxnews, MSNBC, and CNN that perpetuate the same type of negative discourse as Crossfire. To quote Stewart, "It's hurting America." I would add that it is hurting your company or organization. While these shows focus primarily on political topics, the impact goes well beyond the ballot booth. What Begala and Carlson revel in-fighting and arguing-is, sadly, entertainment, that is watched by millions. And, of those millions, many work with you every day.

Richard Jackson Harris, in his book, A Cognitive Psychology of Mass Communication, writes that "in an interesting study of perceived partisanship of news sources, Coe, et. al., found that liberal partisans saw more bias in the traditionally conservative sources like *Fox News* or the *O'Reilly Factor*, while conservatives saw more bias in *The Daily Show*. In other words, we see bias in sources that we strongly disagree with and fail to notice biases consistent with our own[38]. Not only that, people seek out news sources which they believe to be ideologically compatible with themselves, even on topics not particularly prone to partisan bias, such as crime reports or travel stories."[39]

Researchers Iyanger and Hahn add that "It is no mere coincidence that the trend toward a more divided electorate has occurred simultaneously with the revolution in information technology. Forty years ago, the great majority of Americans got their daily news from one of three network newscasts. These newscasts offered a homogeneous and generic "point–counterpoint" perspective on the news, thus ensuring that exposure to the news was a common experience. The development of cable television and the explosion of media outlets on the Internet have created a more fragmented information environment in which cable news, talk radio, and 24-hour news outlets compete for attention. Consumers can access—with minimal effort— newspapers, radio, and television stations the world over. Given this dramatic increase in the number of available news outlets, it is not surprising that media choices increasingly reflect partisan considerations. People who feel strongly about the correctness of their cause or policy preferences seek out information they believe is consistent rather than inconsistent with their preferences."[40]

So politics and cable news are to blame for our innovation problems? Not exactly. However, if this is what people watch and what people begin to model, how can we be surprised that ideas struggle to gain traction in an organization when, as the research shows, that "people who feel strongly about the correctness of their cause or policy preferences seek out information they believe is consistent rather than inconsistent with their preferences." It could be argued that this is the *OPPOSITE* of innovation and creativity.

What is playing out on TV, the web, and social media is seeping into the behaviors of members of our society, i.e. *employees*. According to Nielsen Research, the average American watches more than 5 hours of television each day.[41] Add in social media, video games, and internet use and the number is staggering. "That won't work." "You are wrong and I am right." "The problem with that is." "Yeah but." "That's a dumb idea." All of these statements have proliferated the airways and are considered 'normal' by today's standards. While this book can't change the media, it can enable a person to reflect on his or her own behaviors and mindset, recognize one's own negativity and the sources of such thought patterns and reactions (school, the media, others in society, etc.) and begin to make a conscious effort to shift one's thinking.

Here are few exercises to help you begin to recognize how you might be reacting to ideas and where you are experiencing negativity that could be influencing your behaviors. This is not a judgment on anyone or a 'gotch ya' exercise. This is simple to help you get through step 1-recognizing just how much influence negativity has over the innovative process. Complete these and then let's move on to moving from recognizing the power of negativity to embracing and embedding the simple behaviors that comprise a POP! Culture into your organization.

1. Watch 1 hour of a cable TV news program, ideally one such as Crossfire where the show is designed to foster "debate." What did you notice when ideas were suggested?

   _____

   _____

   _____

2. Watch another cable TV news program that is known to be partisan (i.e. very Republican or very Democrat). What did you notice? How do one's biases influence a discussion, especially when ideas are explored?

   _____

   _____

   _____

3. Spend one day tallying how many times you hear the phrases below. What have you learned? Circle

the tallies when you said one of the phrases. Where did you notice these phrases (work, home, TV, radio, web, etc.)

Negative phrases	Positive phrases
• Yeah but... • The problem with that is... • That won't work because... • That's a bad idea, but....	• Yes and... • That's interesting. Tell me more... • Help me understand... • That's a great idea...
Number of times you heard these or ones like them (use a tally mark)	Number of times you heard these or ones like them (use a tally mark)

With respect to how this is playing out in the workplace, Sandra Robinson at the University of British Columbia writes that:

"O'Leary-Kelly and colleagues (1996) used Bandura's (1977) social learning perspective to examine factors that encourage antisocial behavior."[42] (NOTE: Anti-social behavior is behavior that lacks consideration for others

and may cause damage to the society, whether intentionally or through negligence. This is the opposite of pro-social behavior, which helps or benefits the society).[43]

She adds that *"one such factor was the presence of role models within a work context. They argued that if individuals work in environments that include others who serve as models for antisocial behavior, these individuals are more likely themselves to behave in antisocial ways. When individuals operate within group settings, they are typically able to observe other group members, which creates the opportunity for these members to serve as models. In addition, Bandura's research on disengagement of moral control suggests that diffusion of responsibility, a common outcome in group contexts, can lead individuals to disconnect the self-regulatory systems that typically govern moral conduct*[44]. *A group's climate reflects the aggregate perceptions of group members regarding a particular aspect of the work setting, perceptions that influence the types of behaviors that are exhibited within the group. When there is strong similarity in members' perceptions and behaviors, the social context is most potent and thus most capable of having a profound influence on member behavior. Therefore, we expected that the degree of similarity in group members' levels of antisocial behavior would moderate the extent to which a group's general level of antisocial behavior would influence an individual group member's level."*

Finally, she shares that *"Salancik and Pfeffer[44] posited that the effect of a particular social environment on individual attitudes and behavior depends on the degree to which there are shared beliefs within the social environment. Social learning theory also would be consistent with this moderating effect. As argued above, the antisocial behavior of individual group members may be influenced by the role models they encounter within a group. To the extent that potential role models exhibit similar levels of antisocial behavior, there is a stronger probability that the individual member will choose a role model that reflects the group's norms. For example, if most members of a work group behave in antisocial ways, the likelihood that a new group member might choose a role model who exhibits antisocial behavior is increased, and the chance that the newcomer will develop antisocial actions is also greater."*[45]

In other words-Monkey See, Monkey Do.

One other item I am compelled to introduce when discussing negativity is 'the typo.' I get some push back on this so I expect that you may not initially agree with the position I am about to present. A typo-in a resume, a document, an email-is often seen as a signal of a world ending collapse that indicates impending doom and destruction for the person responsible for such a horrendous mistake. "How dare you write a 200 page document and misspell one word!" People collapse in the street, pounding their fists as they cry out, "why, why?" The reaction to a typo conjures up images of royalty turning their noses with such contempt and disgust. "Away with you! We have no time for your ineptness." It is amazing how righteous we become when we find a mistake. In fact, I have seen and heard some of the most outrageous stories when it comes to typos. My favorite is a senior leader actually stopping a conference call where the topic was a multimillion dollar project because one word was spelled incorrectly. "I am not your proof reader," he said. "Reschedule when you are actually ready." Slam. Down with the phone. Meeting over.

Now, what's the point? Really. Because a person typed one letter in a document of thirty pages we grind everything to a halt? This is ludicrous. Just to be clear, I am not advocating including typos in documents or being lazy and not proof reading one's material. But-news flash-people do make mistakes.

The typo represents our obsession with negativity. We could be presented with an outstanding piece of work and, rather than focus on all of the positive aspects of the effort and all of the hard work someone or a team has completed, we instead focus on a tiny, miniscule mistake and shatter the entire project. Yes, if the mistake was indeed huge and led to a medical mistake or a problem with an engineering design that affected people's lives then the criticism is well warranted. However, most of us on a day to day basis do not deal with life and death situations that result is terrible outcomes if, for example, we type an 'n' instead of an 'm.'

Imagine for a minute that when the United States Constitution was about to be signed someone proof read it and found some typos. "That's it! Forget the whole thing. Shut the country down and reschedule the Convention until you are ready." Well, guess what? There are typos in the US Constitution. The U.S. Archives writes that "As the members of the Convention prepared to sign the document, Hamilton took up a position beside the last of the four sheets, laid out for signing, and appears to have taken charge of the process as the delegates from each state came forward to sign. In this capacity, he wrote the name of each state at the left of the growing column of signatures. When he came to the largest state delegation, headed by Benjamin Franklin, he wrote "Pensylvania." And thus the parchment reads today."[46]

Did Ben say 'scrap the whole thing?' No, he signed and we moved forward as country. He's was still probably ticked the eagle was chosen over the turkey as the national bird but, like the typo, he got over it.

Since we are discussing important documents and literary works, how about we discuss the Bible for a moment. A version of the Bible printed in 1631 stated that "thou shalt commit adultery." Imagine going to the library and opening up to that page. A life changer for some I am sure. "But honey, look, I was just following what it said in the Bible."

I challenge you when you come across a typo to ask yourself if your reaction is commensurate with the impact of the mistake. My guess is most likely it is not, and, instead it is a reflection of how obsessed we have become as a society with negativity.

Chapter 9

Schools need a lesson on innovation

"Imagination is everything. It is the preview of life's coming attractions."

— Albert Einstein

Let's step away from the workplace and revisit schools for a moment. Maria Westling Allodi, in a 2009 edition of Springer's Science and Business Media[47] writes that "Creating something involves self-affirmation and fulfillment. The creative product gives feedback about one's own identity: it mirrors a symbolic image of the self. The person feels not only defined from the outside, but can define herself. In many school situations, the pupils are in fact defined from outside and their performance is evaluated in relation to external criteria, standards or norms." She adds that, "extrinsic motivation and competition seem to affect creative performance negatively[48].

The answer to creating an innovative work culture may lie in building an innovative *school* culture. In addition, parents need to examine their behaviors and the media that they allow their children to consume. We go to school and, as we have seen, the creativity in us begins to erode. As we grow we watch and read media that promotes negative and antisocial behaviors. Upon leaving school we enter the workplace and those behaviors accompany us. And the cycle goes around and around, with the result being a climate and culture that, in effect, is crushing innovation. It is imperative that we expand our discussion beyond the workplace and include schools as well. If we are able to seize the opportunity to move further back in the process, i.e. working with people before they enter the workforce, then creating innovative work environments will be that much easier. In addition, adults need to pay careful attention to the words they use, the behaviors they model, and the information to which they allow children access.[49] If we, as a society, community, country, or even a global entity, want to begin to solve some of our most pressing issues, we need to look to the words of Jon Stewart-"Why do we have to fight? It's hurting America. Stop, stop, stop, stop hurting America." Healthy debate and healthy competition can be productive. I would argue that much of the activity and discourse around debate and competition has become destructive.

In a 1961 study, Albert Bandura conducted a study in which a child sat in a playroom with an adult who either a) played peacefully in the corner or who b) aggressively beat a five-foot inflatable clown doll named Bobo. The child then followed the experimenter to a second playroom where he or she was intentionally frustrated by not allowing him or her to play with certain toys. The child was then escorted to a third room and left to play alone for twenty minutes. Each child's behavior was carefully recorded in five-second intervals. Among the toys in this experimental room was a three-foot inflatable Bobo doll. Children who had been exposed to the nonaggressive situation generally played peacefully and were rarely aggressive toward the doll. However, those who had witnessed aggression often imitated that aggression. Like the adult models, boys and girls in the aggressive condition beat and yelled at Bobo. Compared to the children in the nonaggressive condition, these children also spent 50 percent less time sitting and playing quietly.[50]

In other words, our children-our future workforce-are watching. And, I would all propose that your employees and associates are watching you as well. As illustrated in the Bobo experiment, behavior may not be genetic, *it may be learned.*

One of the best examples of this hypothesis is the 1988 movie, *Big*, with Tom Hanks. In the movie, a 12-year-old makes a wish to be big and, to his surprise, awakens the next morning to find he is now a man in his late 20's/early 30's. That man is played by Tom Hanks. *Big* is interesting on so many levels (and we will explore the movie in more detail later in the book) but there is one particularly lesson –much of our behavior is learned through social interactions. For example, Hanks' character becomes an executive at a toy company. Why? Because, although physically he is a grown man, emotionally he is still 12-years-old (no one knows this). He, in effect, has the mind of the child and is able to envision ideas for toys and games that adults simply can't. But something interesting happens. As the movie progresses Hanks starts to become emotionally big as well. While at first had he no idea what a marketing report was or what was considered 'proper' etiquette, he soon finds himself acting and behaving just as the other workers at the company do, going so far as to begin to ignore his best friend, work long hours, and focus on profits over fun. The environment has completely changed him.

Yes, *Big* is simply a movie, but it does force the question, 'what happens to us as we get older-why do we lose that innocence and creativity?' As we have discussed, we *learn* to lose some of our best qualities, especially the ones essential to innovation. The good news is we can unlearn and relearn as we will see in chapter four.

As I mentioned earlier, I am a parent of two young children. Interestingly, I have noticed them asking more frequently to 'check my phone to see the weather' and needing to 'look some stuff on the internet.' Why? Because that is what *my wife and I* do. Extrapolate those examples to include diet, choice of language, watching TV, working hard, etc. and the pattern is clear. And, as illustrated by research, the trend continues right into the workplace, resulting in antisocial behaviors and those that 'lack consideration for others.' A POP! Culture is one way to change the trajectory on which we have placed our children and have encouraged our employees to follow. Hopefully by simply reading this chapter you are now aware of just how widespread and impeding of innovation negative behaviors can be and the dire need to change one's thinking.

Chapter 10

The power of yes

"Security is mostly a superstition. Life is either a daring adventure or nothing."-Helen Keller

Now that we all recognize just how negative the world around us can be-and possibly ourselves as well-it is time to move in the realm of the positive.

CNN had a program on recently that showcased three high schools in different parts of the United States. Each was participating in an interactive robotics competition.

School one was from an affluent community. School two was from a middle of the road community. School three was from an underserved community. Guess who went the farthest in the competition? The underserved community. Why? Because they had what they called their 'secret weapon.'

The program explained that their secret weapon was building an identical robot with which they could use to practice for 30 days after their official machine had been packaged, shipped, and submitted.

The real secret weapon? *THE IDEA* to build a second identical robot.

In a blinding flash of the obvious the team said, 'hey wait, the key to winning is not the robot but being able to maneuver and work the robot.' So, while everyone else was focused on complex physics problems and mechanics, they also got creative from a team and process perspective. BRILLIANT.

This is a great lesson to everyone. When it appears you may be at a competitive disadvantage, EVERYONE can think of ideas, which by the way, cost the same regardless of economic situations. They are FREE.

"Yes and" versus "Yeah but"

While we are on the topic of schools, let's explore another great example of innovative thinking. What if I told you that schools all across America could dramatically reduce their drop-out rates and increase graduation rates to 100%. Yes, 100%. Just to put this in perspective, the current drop-out rate in the United States is approximately 7% and in some states the graduation rate is between 62% and 67%.[51] Taylor County School District in Campbellsville, Kentucky, has developed an innovative and radical approach to education. Taylor County Superintendent, Roger D. Cook, has led the implementation of a system that, as he describes:

> *Imagine, if you can, a school where students do not have specific teachers assigned to them, nor do teachers have specific students on their roster.*
>
> *Imagine a school where students come each day with a list of standards to work on and accomplish—right when they walk in the door. They can go to the teacher of their choice in order to accomplish the completion of these standards. Or, they can do them on their own in any setting they wish, as long as they maintain accomplishing the minimum amount of standards in a minimum amount of time. Some students, for example, may work individually in the media center not having to go to any classroom.*
>
> *And last but not least, imagine a district at large where the dropout rate is at zero percent.*

In this type of environment, students would come and go as they please, but would be required to prove the successful completion of work and pass assessments to demonstrate understanding.

I am in my ninth year of promoting performance-based education, and my excitement about personalizing learning for students based on their mental capacity, rather than chronological, age is at an optimum level. In the Taylor County School District, we have created a self-paced, anytime/anywhere learning environment and our students are accelerating through their courses at a rate they choose.

We have had up to 300 elementary school students bussed to our middle school to take upper-level course work. We have over 500 high school credits earned at our middle school each year, and we are graduating many seniors as mid-term sophomores in college. Students are able to complete course work 24 hours-per-day, seven days-per-week and 365 days during the year.

Bottom line? Students are not restricted by how many courses they are allowed to attempt or when they can take the courses.[52]

There are probably one of two reactions to this information going through your mind right now. The first is "Wow, this is great! How can we help take this idea and the associated successful results to other parts of America?" The second, however, is most likely the reaction most people will have. Are you ready? Brace yourself but here it comes, like a huge anvil in a Bugs Bunny cartoon falling from the sky, ready to crush all the enthusiasm and energy that are producing *PROVEN AND MEASURABLE RESULTS*. The second reaction probably looks and sounds something like this: "Yeah but, he can do this because...." Or "The problem with this approach is...." Or "That wouldn't work here because..." OR-and this is my favorite-"That's crazy and stupid and won't work."

What do you think? Am I off base here? Based on my years and years of experience, I am confident I am not too far off. It is not like I invented those phrases or tried to paint a picture of a far-fetched and implausible reaction. This second reaction happens every day all across businesses, schools, homes, churches-everywhere.

What if, instead, we changed the 'yeah but' to a 'yes and.' YES AND, we could include community service initiatives in this approach. YES AND, those community service projects could include tutoring students all over the world using technology. YES AND, by tutoring people all over the world the students in Kentucky would start to develop a global perspective and think on a grander scale. YES AND....YES AND...YES AND.

In a recent New York Times interview, venture capitalist CEO of CueBall, Tony Tjan, offers this suggestion:

> *When someone gives you an idea, try to wait just 24 seconds before criticizing it. If you can do that, wait 24 minutes. Then if you become a Zen master of optimism, you could wait a day, and **spend that time thinking about why something actually might work**.*[53]

My belief is that ideas are gifts, and, like any time you receive a gift, you (hopefully) respond with respect and thankfulness. "Oh, thank you so much for the baked bean processor, I can't wait to use it." Even if you hate beans, are allergic to beans, or lost your life savings in a horrible bean factory investment scheme, you still say "thank you." Also, how many of us still have gifts-some of which we couldn't even identify when we received them, stored somewhere in an attic or basement. Why keep them? Why respond nicely? The answer is obvious-we want to be considerate of people's feelings. Someone has taken the time to get you something that they thought you would like. How dare you disrespectfully dismiss the gift as worthless, stupid, or any other adjective that would hurt the person? If we do this with gifts we don't like or even know what they are, then why do we do react so negatively to ideas? IDEAS ARE GIFTS. Someone has taken the time and energy to share something with you-embrace it, build on it, and be respectful in along the way. Imagine someone name Moe gave you a gift for your birthday and, right in front of him, you laughed at him, told him that his idea was dumb, and tossed the gift aside. Fast forward a year later to your next birthday. You go through your gifts and you notice there is not one from Moe. You are furious. "He didn't even get me a gift" you resentfully mutter under your breath. And why should he since you will probably just discard it as worthless? Let's now play this out at work or in school. A person named Larry tosses out an idea (a gift) and it is met with 'yeah but,' 'the problem with that is,' or 'that's a dumb idea (gift).' He quietly retreats and backs down. But, instead, he doesn't give up on the idea (gift), he simply takes it back and puts it to use-and you read about him in Fortune Magazine one day.

Another great example is the 1988 hit movie *Big* with Tom Hanks. Hanks plays the part of a kid named Josh who becomes an adult when he 'wishes he was big.' In the body of a 30 year-old man, he has the mind of a 13 year-old. As only Hollywood could write the script, he becomes the VP of Product Development at a leading toy company in a matter of days. In a classic scene, there is a meeting at which actor John Heard, playing the part of a mean, corporate manager, lays out a strategy for a new product. Hanks, in his 13 year-old mind, innocently offers some other options and the group begins to get energy behind some of his suggestions. John Heard, in a desperate act of trying to maintain control rather than go with the flow, begins to physically try to end the meeting and stop the discussion. Why would he do this when the group is so energized? Why not let the idea explosion continue? Why not just simply say 'thank you for this great gift' and build on it? The result was Hanks' idea resonates with everyone in the room, including the CEO. As the CEO says, "well done Josh, well done."

If you have ever been to an improvisational comedy show or watched the TV program Whose Line Is It Anyway? Then you have seen 'yes and' in action. It is the tenant of improv comedy. While I have great admiration for improv performers (I have done some myself), I do not subscribe to the idea that by simply getting everyone to say 'yes and' is the answer to creating an innovative culture. It is just one piece to the puzzle. As I will discuss as we go on, there are other things that need to be done to alter people's mindset to help them share, build on, evaluate, prioritize, and DO SOMETHING with ideas.

Chapter 11

*A little more from science
on the matter at hand*

*"What if you mix the mayonnaise in the can, WITH the tuna
fish? Or... hold it! Chuck! I got it! Take LIVE tuna fish, and FEED
'em mayonnaise! Oh this is great."-Michael Keaton in the movie
Night Shift*

Let's pause for a moment and revisit what science has to say about all of this. There are five areas that have a dramatic effect on innovation we will explore in more detail. They are:

- Psychological Safety
- Uncertainty Avoidance
- Functional Fixedness
- Evaluation Apprehension
- Risk Aversion

Psychological Safety

There is quite a bit of emphasis, and rightfully so, in organizations around physical safety. In the United States we have OSHA (The Organizational Safety and Health Administration) which is a part of the Department of Labor that works to ensure that American employees are afforded safe working conditions. In addition, many companies, particularly those involved in manufacturing or where complex machinery is involved, have what are called 'safety moments.' Safety moments provide employees to call attention to something they have seen or experienced that could lead to an accident. In fact, some companies require a safety moment at various points in the day as a way to prevent injuries. However, while there is no question that physical safety is critical, there is another aspect to safety that may be just as important. Psychological Safety.

Psychological safety is a shared belief that the team is safe for interpersonal risk taking.[67] In psychologically safe teams, team members feel accepted and respected. It is also the most studied enabling condition in group dynamics and team learning research.[68]

When team members are motivated at work and want to share an idea for improving performance, **they frequently do not speak up because they fear that they will be harshly judged.** When psychological safety is present, team members think less about the potential negative consequences of expressing a new or different idea than they would otherwise. As a result, they speak up more when they feel psychologically safe and are motivated to improve their team or company. 68

This is a critical point and one that aligns exactly with the mission and philosophy of why innovation is easy. If a company creates an environment of Psychological Safety then, as stated above, "team members think less about the potential negative consequences of expressing a new or different idea than they would otherwise." In other words, make it safe for people to share ideas and the will work to improve your organization. If someone does not feel safe then the ideas never come out. Sound too easy? It's not.

Recently Google asked the question, "what makes the perfect team?" After years of research and volumes of data, they concluded that the most critical component to a good team was-wait for it-Psychological Safety. So, while you may be skeptical of anything I have written in this book or the overall philosophy I am trying to convey, can you really be skeptical of Google? What Google has learned is exactly what The Innovation Company attempts to do with companies and organizations. We even take a few steps further.

Uncertainty Avoidance

Uncertainty Avoidance is a term created as a result of the research of Geert Hofstede.[54] Basically, the more a culture dislikes uncertainty or ambiguity, the more rules or structure are put in place. Hofstede would recognize a culture such as this as having a High Uncertainty Index. Conversely, the more comfortable a culture is with uncertainty and ambiguity, the less rules and structure are put in place. This would signal a Low Uncertainty Index. How does this relate to innovation and creativity? If your organization and culture is one that can't comprehend the thought of someone questioning company policy, well, you can see guess where that might lead. I once worked for a company that had the following organizational hierarchy: The Project Analyst reported to the Project Manager who reported to (and I couldn't make this up) the Manager of Project Management who reported to the Director of Project Management. We spent countless hours on documentation, sign-offs, and status meetings? Was this a pharmaceutical company or military operation where lives were at stake? No. We managed people's health benefits. One time, so fed up with all the ludicrous work environment, I decided to run an experiment. One of my tasks was to review a weekly 50 page data base report and then sign and approve the work. The database analyst brought me the report and asked me to review it and have it back to him by the end of the week. "Who has more experience with data base, you or me?" I asked him. He humbly smiled, knowing it was he who had much more knowledge than I did. "I am assuming that you did this report the same way you have done the other hundred or so you have done." I then took the pen and signed the report and gave it back to him. "Done," I said. He looked stunned. "Bill [I have changed his name], why in my right mind would I waste hours of my life doing this task when there is no need." Now, Bill was smart enough to know this would be our little secret since he too understood the culture in which we worked. And week after week, while my counterparts slowly increased their eyeglass prescriptions pouring over nonsensical bits of information, I was busy heading home on time.

I often signed credit card receipts as Elvis Presley or Jimi Hendrix and expense reports as Joe DiMaggio or Mickey Mantle. Sometimes, when I had to document who joined me for a business dinner, I picked a theme like 'actors' and list Tom Hanks, Jack Nicholson, and John Travolta. And guess what, no one ever checked. Ironically, in this company's effort to implement controls and avoid uncertainty, they were actually inspiring my creativity.

Functional Fixedness

For example, earlier I mentioned author and speaker Daniel Pink. In his book *Drive*, he provides an example of what is known as Functional Fixedness. In the 1930's psychologist Karl Duncker defined Functional Fixedness as being a "mental block against using an object in a new way that is required to solve a problem."[55] Duncker devised an experiment where participants were given a candle, a box full of tacks, and a book of matches. The challenge presented was to attach the candle to the wall so that the wax doesn't drip on the table. Many people begin by trying to tack the candle to the wall. But that doesn't work. Some light a match, melt the side of the candle, and try to adhere it to the wall. That doesn't work either. But after five or ten minutes, most people stumble onto the solution which is to tack the box to the wall and then light the candle.[56] While this may not seem revolutionary and ground breaking, it has tremendous application to the realm of innovation. If I were to ask you to tell me what you use baking soda for in your home you most likely are not going to say 'for baking.' I would suspect that you may say 'to keep my refrigerator smelling fresh' or 'it is in my toothpaste.' This is a perfect of how smashing through functional fixedness can have a profound impact on a company-or any organization for that matter. Arm & Hammer, a company almost synonymous with baking soda, did not start marketing the product for cleaning purposes *until after 50 years* of promoting it as a leavening agent. The company did not need to invent something new, buy entry into a new market, or expand away from its core offerings. It simply overcame Functional Fixedness and the rest is history.

Evaluation Apprehension

Another psychological theory that affects innovation and creativity is Evaluation apprehension. Evaluation apprehension refers to the experience of being anxious about being negatively evaluated or not positively evaluated. In other words it is the concern for how others are evaluating us.[57] While this term applies largely to experiments in which human being participate, it is also relevant to innovation and creativity. Think back to our discussion around the Butter Fly Effect and Chaos Theory in which we saw how a one seemingly benign action-reacting negatively to an idea-can have enormous and widespread effects and consequences. In addition to helping individuals overcome functional fixedness, organizations need to create an environment that minimizes Evaluation Apprehension, or, more simply put, help people feel safe to share and express their ideas and creative impulses. If someone is operating from a place of fear-fear of being judged negatively, laughed or, my favorite, being laughed at, how can an organization possibly expect people to come forward with innovative ideas? They can't. And, as I stated before, this is not my opinion. Evaluation Apprehension is grounded in scientific research and is proven to impact the environment in which people work, learn, or live. The good news? A POP! Culture addresses this issue.

Risk Aversion

On the heel of Evaluation Apprehension is risk. BlessingWhite, a Princeton-based consultancy, asked employees whether they are encouraged to take risks. To little surprise, only 26% of employees said they are often encouraged to take risks. A startling 41% said they are never asked to do so.[58] Reversing the culture to allow innovation or encouraging candor is a huge barrier for many organizations. Many risk takers and outspoken staff members are sanctioned or even fired for breaching the corporate norms. And many leaders would be hard pressed to cite an occasion where they praised an employee's willingness to take a chance.[58] In summary, groups that are risk averse will inhibit radical innovation (Ekvall, 1996).[59] However, an informal, open, and inquiring environment that values experimentation, with leaders promoting innovation by creating a shared belief that team members are safe to take interpersonal risks will facilitate radical innovation (Claver, Llopis et al, 1998)[60]

Do you promote risk? Do you celebrate risk? Do you ever publicly recognize someone for taking a risk, even if the results may be perceived as failure? Or, do you, like most individuals, primarily celebrate success and achievement? In my twenty plus years of working, I have yet to see a leader stand up and say, "we are here today to recognize Ed in Accounting for taking a risk and totally failing." It may happen, but not very often. What does happen is that Ed from Accounting is searching for a new job while everyone else in the company is now scared to death to step even a tiny bit outside the lines.

While studying electrical engineering I recall a very profound statement by one of my professors. "If you are not comfortable with trial and error then this major may not be for you." As a parent this is something I have become increasingly concerned about as I constantly see children over protected from failure by their parents. The right grades, at the right school, to get the right job, and the right company, in the right field. In classrooms and on playing fields children are so over coached and influenced by adults that it is no wonder that they have perfect grades and test scores. But there is a price that is being paid for this 'perfection.' All the topics discussed above-Uncertainty Avoidance, Functional Fixedness, Evaluation Apprehension, and Risk Aversion-are about to exponentially explode as our current students become more and more a part of the workforce. While working with a client, there was a team that was asked to give a 45 minute presentation. "What is the best way to do this?" I was asked. "Just use your best judgment," I replied. "But, should it be 30 minutes for presenting and 15 minutes for questions or half and half?" "Just use your best judgment," I stressed. "What is the way groups have done the best at this assignment divided things up in the past?" they asked. Finally, knowing the answer to the question I was about to ask, I approached one of the members of the team. "What was your grade point average in college?" "4.0" the person responded in a soft voice. "Have you ever failed at anything?" I asked. The answer was an embarrassing "no." Why was this person embarrassed rather than proud? Because he knew what was happening. He could follow all the rules and obtain a perfect score-but the game had changed. No longer was it about being perfect. In fact, it was just the opposite. He was now being asked to challenge assumptions, develop creative solutions, and think differently-and he was floundering.

There is one particular group that is not influenced at all by any of the barriers to innovation discussed previously-stand-up comics. Years ago I decided to take a class in stand-up comedy and, since then, have tremendous admiration for anyone in this field. I had read that some business schools were requiring students to take stand-up comedy classes under the premise that if someone could do that, they would never be scared of any presentation. Having had to perform twice, I can attest to the truth behind this theory. I sincerely think that I will never be as nervous as I was on each of those two evenings. I will also never feel as exhilarated as I did following each set. While I learned the obvious-self-confidence, overcoming fears, basic performing skills-there was one piece of knowledge that was life changing. The instructor told us that for even the best comedians only about 60% of their material works. That means in a five minute set only about three minutes will be considered funny-*for the best comics*. Stand-up comics get up on stage-alone-night after night and let it fly. They deal with hecklers, silence, and immediate feedback that it really good or really, really bad. And they keep getting up and doing it over and over again. Which brings us to possibly the greatest example of innovation ever.

Chapter 12

The show about nothing

"The man with a new idea is a crank-until the idea succeeds."-

Mark Twain

Waiting for a table in a Chinese restaurant. Forgetting when you left your car in parking garage. Taking a dessert out of the trash and eating it. Who could predict that these story lines and the hundreds more would result in one of the greatest and most successful television shows in history-*Seinfeld*.

In Seinfeld's fourth season there is an episode where Jerry Seinfeld and his friend, George Costanza, are sitting in a coffee shop. Here is an excerpt of the dialogue as written in the script:

> GEORGE: Why don't they have salsa on the table?
>
> JERRY: What do you need salsa for?
>
> GEORGE: Salsa is now the number one condiment in America.

JERRY: You know why? Because people like to say "salsa." "Excuse me, do you have salsa?" "We need more salsa." "Where is the salsa? No salsa?"

GEORGE: You know it must be impossible for a Spanish person to order seltzer and not get salsa. (Angry) "I wanted seltzer, not salsa."

JERRY: "Don't you know the difference between seltzer and salsa?? You have the seltzer after the salsa!"

GEORGE: See, this should be a show. This is the show.

JERRY: What?

GEORGE: This. Just talking.

JERRY: (dismissing) Yeah, right.

GEORGE: I'm really serious. I think that's a good idea.

JERRY: Just talking? Well what's the show about?

GEORGE: It's about nothing.

JERRY: No story?

GEORGE: No forget the story.

JERRY: You've got to have a story.

GEORGE: Who says you gotta have a story? Remember when we were waiting for, for that table in that Chinese restaurant that time? That could be a TV show.

GEORGE: Yeah. I think we really got something here.

JERRY: What do we got?

GEORGE: An idea.

JERRY: What idea?

GEORGE: An idea for the show.

JERRY: I still don't know what the idea is.

GEORGE: It's about nothing.

JERRY: Right.

GEORGE: Everybody's doing something, we'll do nothing.

JERRY: So, we go into NBC, we tell them we've got an idea for a show about nothing.

GEORGE: Exactly.

JERRY: They say, "What's your show about?" I say, "Nothing."

GEORGE: There you go.

(A moment passes)

JERRY: (Nodding) I think you may have something there.

While in reality the pitch Jerry Seinfeld gave to NBC was not actually for a show about nothing but, rather, a show about how a comedian gets his material, let's use the conversation in the script since it was the style and approach the show took on as it was produced. Regardless, the exchange between Jerry and George is a perfect example of how being open to an idea, exploring the idea, and feeling safe to even share the idea in the first place is critical. Seinfeld didn't dismiss or crush the idea for a 'show about nothing.' He listened. He asked questions. He sought to understand. He obtained clarity. Then, and only then, did he pass judgment and, in this case, if was affirming George's idea.

Imagine if he had responded with "that's dumb" or "that's stupid" or "yeah but" or "the problem with that is" or "that won't work because." The idea dies and, in this scenario, the show dies. Just to put this in perspective, the show *Seinfeld* is worth billions of dollars-that's billions with a b. So, maybe George and Jerry are on to something.

Chapter 13

I have a NEWIDEA-embedding key behaviors

"Our best ideas come from clerks and stockboys."-Sam Walton

So how do we put this POP! Culture into motion? The good news it is very simple. While much of my work involves conducting talks or workshops with groups of individuals from one or many organizations, these engagements are usually only about 60 to 90 minutes in length. In fact, some people 'get it' simply by hearing the story about the title of the book. Then, after doing some very simple exercises and discussing many of the topics I have outlined in the previous chapters, I introduce the following process: NEWIDEA.

NEWIDEA is a simple process to take a thought from an idea to action, where the action may be to do nothing at all with the idea. This is very important point to make since it is critical that everyone understand that just because an idea is suggested does NOT mean it will be implemented. The goal is not to say yes to every idea or to build on every idea. It is simply to be open to ideas and to respect others for their input. That's what a POP! Culture is. Openness and respect. Openness and respect. That's what this process does, especially in the first three steps. By having a POP! Culture, people will not expect every idea to be acted upon. The combination of a POP! Culture and the NEWIDEA! process encourages people to keep 'throwing out the ideas' without concern of any of the research we have covered so far.

N – No negativity!

E – Encourage the
    person

W – Wait…and LISTEN!

I – Include input

D – Document the
    idea

E – Evaluate and
    explore options

A – Action!

Does every idea have to go through the NEWIDEA process? The answer is no. What I tell people is that if you are able to get your folks to model N, E, and W, you are 90% of the way to achieving great things. I describe this process as being 'situational,' meaning that the situation will determine how far along the process you will travel.

For example, let's say a friend of mine and I are on a subway talking about our jobs and I say I have an idea. I don't expect him to say, "hold on, we better get off at the next stop and get a flipchart and some markers so we can write the idea down." That would be crazy. At the same time, if my friend and I are meeting with the Board of Directors and we are trying to come up with ideas for the strategic direction for the next three years, a flipchart and some markers may not be a bad idea. Low structure-make sure to get through N-E-W. High structure, pull out the flipchart and go all the way to A-Action.

Here is example of how the NEWIDEA! process can work. I was conducting a workshop with a leading global financial services and insurance company. The group I was working with was having a tough time with the perception that their team was a roadblock to getting things done. This was not reality at all. During the workshop we were focusing on the following real life situation: "How can we create a valid perception with filed staff and other departments that we are a necessary and valuable step in the process of serving our customers?"

I told the group they needed to come up with at least two ideas that were 'ridiculous' and 'outrageous.' I do this with groups to show that what is often perceived as ridiculous is often not ridiculous at all. One of the people in the group had written down on a flipchart 'have a circus at our department.' I asked, "is that your ridiculous idea?" She said, "yes" as everyone laughed. I said, "okay, let me show you how using the NEWIDEA! process will take what you think is an outrageous idea and actually show you it is not so outrageous at all."

I said, "Please say your idea again." She said, "let's have a circus at our department." "Great," I said, "This is where we start with N-No negativity." I looked at the group. No laughter. No mocking. No phrases like 'the problem with that is.' "Let's move on to E-Encourage the person. Why do you say let's have a circus?" I asked, also pointing out that I was going to model W-Wait and listen. What she said was outstanding. "A circus is loud, fun and a little crazy. My thought is that if we had a circus going on people would come by and see what all the commotion was about. Then, while they were here, we could show them what we do and explain to them face to face how we fit into the process. Plus, it would be fun and different and they would have a good time and tell their co-workers to go to the circus."

Suddenly 'let's have a circus' didn't seem like such a ridiculous idea. We had gone through N, E, and W and by doing so we had learned something. By being open to an idea, respecting the person for her input, and having a process to follow that promotes innovation and creative thinking, we were on to something. You could see and feel the energy in the room.

"Now let's move on to I-Include input," I said. "How about if I build upon your idea of a circus? What if we have some type of contest or prize for people?" Now people were getting even more excited. "Let's write the idea down," I suggested, moving into D-Document the idea. I wrote down 'let's have a circus' and then to emphasize the power of the NEWIDEA! Process, I crossed it out-with her permission of course. I then wrote 'let's have an event that creates a buzz in the field and in the home office that inspires people to come visit our department so we can then talk with them face to face and show them how we add value.' I asked, "Is this your idea?" "Exactly," she said. "So it's really not about a circus, is it?" I asked. The participants were shaking their heads. I also asked, "where is everyone focused right now?" We were all focused on the flipchart-not on the person who had suggested the idea. Why? Because the idea had been written down.

Another lesson from this story is that 'let's have a circus' was no longer her idea, it was the group's idea. I call this 'Mi idea es su idea'™ or 'My idea is your idea,' where an idea no longer is associated with a person, but has the ownership of the group. I will get back to that in a moment. Continuing with the NEWIDEA! process, we went into E-Explore options and evaluate. I asked, "What tools do you use to help you make group decisions?" My goal here was to use what was already part of their culture. We worked through the idea for a short while and then I said, "Okay, now let's move to A-Action. What should we do from here?" We decided that we would have three people take the idea and all the work we had done, flesh it out further, and come up with a plan within 30 days to present back to the group. Everyone was excited. Note: If by exploring and evaluating options the group decided to take NO action that would have been fine as well.

We weren't having a circus (although I personally think that would be hysterical), we were 'creating a buzz in the field and in the home office that will inspire people to come visit our department so we can then talk with them face to face and show them how we add value.' It wasn't about a circus at all. Imagine if the typical reactions like 'we could never bring an elephant into the building' or 'that would be messy' had come out of people's mouths the second the idea was suggested. The focus would have been on a circus, not on what the person was really trying to say. Everything we had just done was simple and easily transferable to ANY meeting. In a matter of minutes the participants saw the effects of a POP! Culture and the NEWIDEA! process. Everyone now had a common language to share ideas and a simple process to get them to action. Fast, easy, and energizing. The boss was a hero.

The NEWIDEA! process is critical because when someone suggests an idea, it is just that-an idea. The person most likely does not have all the details. The person has usually not had time to completely think it through from A to Z. And often, it is not exactly what the person is really thinking. So, with this in mind, why, when an idea is suggested, do people respond with questions or discouraging comments? What is the harm in simply being open to the idea and respecting the person for their input? None! There will be plenty of time for evaluating and exploring options. This is a critical point. The approach I am suggesting does not mean that healthy debate goes away. What I am proposing is that debate and judgment not be the very first reactions to suggestions or new ideas. My approach is NOT saying 'yes' or 'yes and' to everything-that would be crazy. With a POP! Culture people know that not every idea will be implemented, but that they are in a safe environment to keep tossing out suggestions. Then NEWIDEA! enables them to have a roadmap for ideas to follow. Everyone needs to chill out, take a step back, and let people explain their ideas! Pause. Take a deep breath. Okay, I'm calm now. Let's continue.

Let's get back to this concept of 'Mi idea es su idea'™ or 'My idea is your idea.' We are all so caught up in 'who will get the credit' or 'who will get the recognition' that we often become our own worst enemies. I compare this to an athlete who is more concerned with personal statistics than winning the game. What good is it to be an all-star on a losing team? As mentioned before, ideas are gifts, and, just like gifts, once you hand it over, it ceases to be yours. And that is a good thing. I am firm believer that if you want to get an idea through the system, you have to make people part of the process, give up control, and let others be involved. It has to be their idea. This is part of the reason that people react the way they do when presented with new ideas. It goes back to 'what's in it for me' and 'how will this affect my day-to-day job.'

I often tell people in workshops, particularly managers who are looking to implement a change, that the key is to have the idea come out of their employees' mouths, not the managers' mouths. Buy-in and involvement will increase, resistance will decrease, and more ideas will be implemented. Here is a great quote that someone once shared with me:

> Go with the people.
>
> Live with them.
>
> Learn from them.
>
> Love them.
>
> Start with what they know.
>
> Build with what they have.
>
> And of the best leaders,

when the job is done, the task accomplished,
the people will all say: "We have done this
ourselves."

Lao Tsu, China, 700 b.c.

The next time you have an idea or need to implement a change, try and make it the idea of others, not your idea. Is it credit and recognition you want for your ideas, or for your ideas to be implemented? Maybe you can get both, but is credit really the goal? Think "Mi idea es su idea"™ and you will be amazed at how barriers come down and how many ideas move forward. How about adding this to your Bill of Rights?

Imagine a culture where people know and accept that once an idea is out there or on a flip chart it is no longer their idea but rather the 'ownership' of the group. I put ownership in quotes because I don't want people to think copyrights. Ownership in this case is meant to imply that the *team* owns the idea, not the individual. Plus, I would argue that the satisfaction from giving of yourself and seeing the team succeed will be much greater than any recognition you get-alone.

Chapter 14

But we already do brainstorming

"No idea is so outlandish that it should not be considered."-
Winston Churchill

Brainstorming. This one activity summarizes the dysfunction that is pervasive in our schools, homes, businesses, and just about any other place where more than one person starts to collaborate with another individual. Think about this. We are so dysfunctional as a society that when we have brainstorming sessions we actually have to spend time setting rules around our behaviors. "Don't judge." "Get all the ideas out." "No idea is a bad idea." "Let people talk." "Be respectful." "Build on ideas." What the freaking heck! These rules are the definitions of a POP! Culture. Therefore, imagine if we were able to avoid having to set the ground rules and if the ground rules weren't rules-they were just the way people behaved regardless if a brainstorming session was taking place or not. When we do brainstorming it is almost as if we are publicly acknowledging "OK, we know that we are completely awful when it comes to creating environments where people feel safe to share ideas and where these ideas are met with respect and openness.

With that in mind, we will take the next hour and behave in a respectful way but then go back to being dysfunctional once the session is over. Sound good? OK, let's get creative."

Brainstorming sessions are what I describe as the National Parks of organizations. They are protected spaces that took an act of Congress-literally-to protect us from ourselves. Think about it. Imagine if The Grand Canyon was not protected or Yellowstone was fair game to land developers. We as a society have said, "If we don't designate this land as special we will probably destroy it." We go to the Parks, enjoy the tranquility, peacefulness, and beauty and then get back in our cars and return to traffic, pollution, and tension. My goal here is not to get all political but to point out just how backwards this thinking is. The same is true for brainstorming sessions. We carve out a little slice of time for brainstorming (i.e. create national parks) that represent the way we wish things could be and then quickly get back to the insane culture that simply crushes and destroys innovation and creative thinking. This is preposterous and a flaw of organizations.

The term brainstorming is credited to a famous advertising executive named Alex Osborn, and was popularized in his book *Applied Imagination*.[61] While there are conflicting studies to the usefulness of brainstorming sessions, the premise of Osborn's approach is worth noting. He proposed four rules for these sessions: don't criticize, quantity is wanted, combine and improve suggested ideas, and say all ideas that come to mind, no matter how wild.[62] My question is, why limit this thinking to brainstorming sessions? Why not strive to have this mode of thinking in place regardless of setting? Yes, there needs to be a system for critical thought, decision making, and action, but why does this need to take place in a session. **I argue that innovation is not something that can be scheduled.** Rather, it is something that, due to an environment, i.e. a POP! Culture, it simply happens all the time.

Please do not interpret my statement above to suggest that brainstorming is bad or that sessions such as these should stop. There is tremendous value in people coming together to share ideas, network, and spark creative thoughts in others. My contention is that too often I have seen the 'National Park' syndrome that I described earlier, and that to think a brief diversion from dysfunction toward a safe environment for sixty to ninety minutes will cure the ills of your company is very optimistic thinking.

Rather than put the pressure on to 'be creative' during brainstorming sessions, I am proposing that these meetings simply be an extension of the organization's culture and, rather than focus on idea generation, focus instead on idea networking and sharing, since, as author Steven Johnson writes, "chance favors the connected mind."[63]

Johnson has spent many years researching innovation and, as the title of one of his books asking, 'where do good ideas come from?'[64] Without going into tremendous detail, Johnson stresses the importance of having 'spaces' where 'hunches' can, in effect, incubate over time. Then, as he describes, one of these hunches connects with another hunch and the idea begins to grow and move forward. This, in a very simple way, describes what he calls 'liquid networks.' (There is no way I have done Johnson's outstanding work justice in only a few lines) In a famous TED talk, Johnson states that "We take ideas from other people, from people we've learned from, from people we run into in the coffee shop, and we stitch them together into new forms and we create something new. That's really where innovation happens." He also adds that "almost all of the important breakthrough ideas did not happen alone in the lab, in front of the microscope. They happened at the conference table at the weekly lab meeting, when everybody got together and shared their kind of latest data and findings, oftentimes when people shared the mistakes they were having, the error, the noise in the signal they were discovering. And something about that environment where you have lots of different ideas that are together, different backgrounds, different interests, jostling with each other, bouncing off each other – that environment is, in fact, the environment that leads to innovation."

This is significant. If an organization creates a POP! Culture that fosters constant idea generation, building upon ideas, and listening, they will be primed to establish an environment like the one Johnson describes. If however, a POP! Culture is not present, I would suggest that the full usefulness of such environments will not be realized and thus innovation will never truly be present. Therefore, brainstorming sessions as we currently know them may not be best for your organization. Instead, they can become more collaborative in nature, since idea generation is already taking place on a continuous basis across the enterprise. Brainstorming sessions can now become what Johnson compares to coffee houses-places where people can come to hang out, talk, share, listen, build upon, and collaborate. Structure is lower, no rules need to be shared, and everyone is working toward helping move ideas forward and to action.

Chapter 15

It's OK to judge

"The way to get good ideas is to get lots of ideas and throw the bad ones away."-Linus Pauling

A misperception that people have when I discuss the philosophy and approach outlined in this book is that criticism is not welcomed. This is absolutely not the case. As discussed earlier when reviewing the dialogue between Jon Stewart and the television hosts on CNN, constructive and healthy debate is not just welcomed, it is *needed*. Please don't confuse being open and respectful to new ideas as the same as all ideas are good and will be implemented. This would be a disaster. It is actually imperative that people know that in a POP! Culture that the environment to share and build ideas is safe and welcoming but that not all ideas will be become actionable. It is not feasible nor is it realistic to expect that any thought that is said, written, or jotted down on a sticky note will be blindly accepted and acted upon. However, if the correct environment is established, then more ideas will have the chance to blossom and be implemented. It is a win for everyone. Also, building off of earlier chapters, ideas may be combined, added to, or altered to take completely different forms than when they were first suggested. The point is that people will be more engaged within your organization leading to positive benefits for the company.

Recognizing that it may be difficult to determine which ideas should move forward and which one should be dismissed or saved for later, one simple tool to use the prioritization matrix shown below.

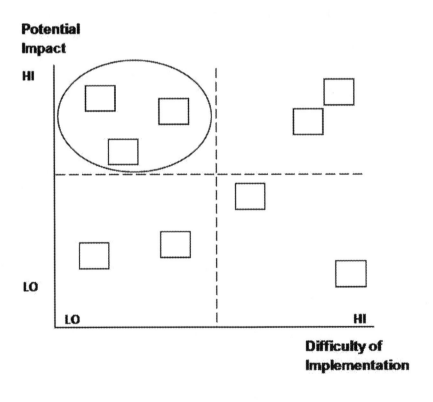

The idea behind a tool like this is to quickly assess which ideas (each written on a sticky note or index card) would have the most impact (the y axis) versus the difficulty to implement (the x axis). With that said, it is up to the team to determine the priority and which ideas-if any-will be acted upon. This matrix is simply an example to start from and the evaluation criteria could change based on the needs of the organization or current circumstances. The bottom line is that the evaluation of ideas is an essential component of the innovation process and, without prioritization or a well thought out method and criteria to determine which ideas stay or go, an organization may find itself with a mountain of great ideas but not many results.

Chapter 16

Show me the money

"Not everything that counts can be counted, and not everything that can be counted counts."-Albert Einstein

The topic of measuring the success of implementing a POP! Culture is one that I struggle with, especially since so much relies on behavioral changes for which there may or may not be a benefit of measuring. For example, I can tell if a person is nice simply by interacting with him or her. I don't need to track how many times he or she said thank you or please over the course of a week, enter the data into Excel, and produce a PowerPoint document with numerous charts and graphs. However, in order to sustain behavioral changes, may be important, especially to show individuals progress toward goals. Measuring the number, value, and actual economic success of newly introduced products by an organization, however, is a somewhat subjective measurement of the organization's innovation capabilities.[65]

There is currently a big push toward 'wearable technology' to help individuals track items such as calories, distance walked, sleep pattern, and other health related information. The Apple Watch or a FitBit are examples of wearable technology. While it may appear that these devices would help people make positive behavioral changes, a recent study by the University of Pennsylvania suggests otherwise. "The gap between recording information and changing behavior is substantial," state the authors in their article, "and while these devices are increasing in popularity, little evidence suggests that they are bridging that gap."[66] The article goes on to state that "Although wearable devices have the potential to facilitate health behavior change, this change might not be driven by these devices alone. Instead, the successful use and potential health benefits related to these devices depend more on the design of the engagement strategies than on the features of their technology. Ultimately, it is the engagement strategies—the combinations of individual encouragement, social competition and collaboration, and effective feedback loops—that connect with human behavior." This article provides important guidance for the creation of a POP! Culture within an organization. It is not enough to simply measure data, share it, and expect change. It is the *engagement strategies* that will be the levers that modify behavior. Therefore, while there may be pieces of information that can help measure the success of a POP! Culture, it is the process by which the environment is created that is essential. In other words, the means are as important as the ends.

Before a measurement process can be implemented an organization must first be clear on what exactly it is that they are measuring. While this may seem obvious, the topic of innovation lends itself to many potential metrics. For example, are we measuring employee engagement? Employee satisfaction? The number of ideas? Financial return on investment? These could all be viable options. The answer to what are we measuring may be different for each organization and may include both qualitative and quantitative data. For example, here are some results that clients have shared with me:

1. A group of 75 accountants and finance managers at a Fortune 500 company, as a client stated, "are generating and implementing great, new ideas on how to better do their jobs and meet the needs of their clients."

2. A team of restaurant general managers at one of the largest food service providers in America indicated that introducing the POP! Culture workshop at the

beginning of an off-site meeting led to tangible actions the team could implement, specifically around an area of concern regarding a process that greatly impacted customers. The client indicated that the session 'primed the pump' and actually made the session productive versus the 'typical unproductive meeting.'

3. Over 100 lawyers working for a multi-billion dollar pharmaceutical company in three different office locations created and implemented a plan to better share information and enhance relationships among the offices to better meet the needs of their internal clients.

4. Team members at a multi-billion dollar insurance and financial services company reported that morale and productivity have greatly increased and that many of the tools taught in the POP! Culture workshop are *used every day*-6 months after the workshops.

5. A prominent utility company initially intended to use the POP! Culture approach with its senior management team. However, due to the impact of the initial efforts, they have expanded the scope of the initiative to include field managers as well.

6. A leader at Fortune 20 company indicated the POP! Culture approach was outstanding and much easier and better than his company's "polluted" process around innovation.

7. A senior manager at a multi-billion auto parts distributor said, "We are doing the NEWIDEA! process and it is so powerful that we have an idea revolution taking place."

8. A team of participants at a well-known newspaper indicated that they "began using what they learned immediately" and that the workshop was "one of the best learning experiences they had ever had." Many are still using what they learned over one year after the workshop.

These results are primarily anecdotal and qualitative in nature. However, *they work for the companies that shared them*-and that is what is important.

In addition to the quotes and examples above, I have worked with clients to create a numeric measure as well. For example, for some clients I conduct a pre and post effort survey of team members to assist with creating a tangible ROI-a number, a chart, a metric. The surveys are created *with* the clients and are designed around *their* goals and objectives. In all cases we collected a combination of quantitative and qualitative data and used it for two purposes. The first was to understand the environment as much as possible *before* implementing a POP! Culture. The second and more obvious was to use the data to determine the effectiveness of the new environment in helping the client meet its business objectives. The questions range from the willingness to share ideas, the responsiveness of leadership and peers, and even the level of passion and accountability in the organization. In one case there was a 37% increase in employees comfort level with sharing new ideas 30 days after an initial workshop. In addition, one client indicated they saw a 90% improvement in productivity around the completion of a particular project.

While these numbers and stories may or may not sound impressive, the important message here is that the only metrics and measurement processes that matter are the ones that are specific to your company. There is no generic approach and, in fact, a process that is not customized to your group may be worthless since what you are trying to measure could be completely different from another team-even in the same company in some cases. The measurements may be around new patents, employee engagement, or possibly completely anecdotal in nature. The key is designing a process and set of data that makes sense, is simple, and will help you with your goals and objectives.

Chapter 17

It's the right thing to do

"If I have a thousand ideas and only one turns out to be good,

I am satisfied."-Alfred Noble

Here is a story that is very touching and shows the power of being open to ideas AND following through. I saw this on ESPN and read about it on ESPN.com.

A former head coach of the Notre Dame football team, Charlie Weis, had visited a very ill 10 year-old child days before a crucial game. In speaking with the child, he asked if there was anything he could do for him and the child gave the coach an idea for the first play of the game. He told Weis to "throw it to the right." The day before the game, the boy passed away. The coach told the team the story and had already talked with his quarterback about the first play.

As fate would have it, Notre Dame's first play came after they recovered a fumble and were backed all the way to their own 1 yard line-99 yards from the other end zone. Logic and the most conservative play calling would result in a hand off and run to try and gain a couple of yards to create a little space for the offense to work. But what about the child's idea? Quarterback Brady Quinn asked the coach, "What are we going to do?" Weis said. "We have no choice. We're throwing it to the right." The play worked and Notre Dame gained 13 yards.

It broke with conventional wisdom. Can you imagine what would have happened if the play had backfired and none of us knew this story? "What a dumb play!" "What a bad idea!" "That's stupid!" All these statements and judgments would have been made-without ever understanding. Openness and respect. Openness and respect. The coach was open to an idea. He respected the idea from the child. Even if the play had 'not worked,' the coach would know inside he had done what was right. But it did work. He let go. He gave up control. He listened. He cared. He followed through. He made the kid's idea the team's idea. Everyone was bought in. He did not fear public opinion. He did not feel the need to sound important and tell the kid 'why the idea wouldn't work.'

If the head coach of Notre Dame football can do this with so much pressure, so much scrutiny, and so much at stake in terms of money and the demands of leading one of the most storied college football teams in history, can we all do what he did? Yes.

While the idea of a POP! Culture is one that can lead to success in your organization, an increase in your bottom line, and better position you to reach your goals and objectives, it really is bigger than all of those things. It is simply the right thing to do. The behaviors encouraged in a POP! Culture will produce results-and they will help bring out the good in everyone. Imagine if, as a society we:

- Listened more
- Judged less
- Were more open to ideas
- Treated people with higher levels of respect
- Encouraged people more
- More willingly shared the credit for successes
- Built people up versus trying to bring them down
- Focused on the positive versus the negative

A POP! Culture is not designed for businesses-it is designed for any environment where people interact and collaborate. Home. Work. School. Church. It does not matter. The principles are the same independent of organization type or setting.

Chapter 18

Putting it all into action

"I am looking for a lot of people who have an infinite capacity to not know what can't be done."-Henry Ford

The science has spoken. The impact of positive versus negative is clear. We even have a way to take ideas from thoughts to action and possibly measuring the impact. The question now is how do you make this happen within your organization, with an organization being a for profit company, a not-for-profit, a school, a church, or even a family or community? The answer is it is easy and it can be as simple or grandiose as you want it to be.

Here are some approaches that are proven to work. Note, for each item in the list below we can work with you or, if you feel comfortable, we can provide you with guidance, facilitator documents, materials lists, and outlines at no cost. The goal is to do what is best for you and your team.

1. Conduct a POP! Culture workshop with a team, group, or even an entire company *just before* an important meeting where you will be needing the brainpower

and ideas of the group to share ideas to address a specific situation or opportunity. We call these Pre-Notes™ since, as opposed to keynotes, they take place before a team meeting, offsite, or, for example, a sales conference. The idea is to quickly get everyone in the proper mindset to maximize the effectiveness of the group's time together.

2. Simply have people read this book and discuss how you can implement the ideas present here in a way that works for your organization. Yes, this is actually proven to work.

3. Conduct a more comprehensive POP! Culture workshop that includes the following:

   a. Generating ideas and creating a plan to embed the NEWIDEA behaviors into our organization in a way that is aligned with the specific nuances of our current culture

   b. Working on a specific real life scenario that your organization or team is facing

   This approach is particularly powerful since it ensures that the time spent during the workshop will be part of a bigger and more sustainable process versus a one-time event. In addition, it encourages more employee buy-in and engagement and has a high likelihood of producing a positive return on investment via the real life scenario.

4. Include a pre and post assessment process to measure key data to assess results.

5. Map out a company-wide initiative that involves all employees at all levels.

Entire company or small group. One time event or a more comprehensive approach. Measure or don't measure. The choice is yours. The idea is to do what is best for your company based on time, resources, and, most importantly, your goals. One thing I do know after doing with a countless number of people-the approach, ideas, and theories discussed in this book work-100% guaranteed.

Chapter 19

Who knew?

And guess what? Mustard really does go on corn! Here is a recipe I found on the Kraft Foods web site. Enjoy! The web address I found this at is http://www.kraftrecipes.com/recipes/mustard-glazed-corn-56758.aspx

2 Tbsp. GREY POUPON Dijon Mustard

2 Tbsp. chopped fresh parsley

1 Tbsp. lemon juice

2 cloves garlic, minced

4 fresh ears of corn, husks and silk removed

1 Tbsp. olive oil

PREHEAT grill on medium heat. Combine mustard, lemon juice, parsley and garlic; set aside.

BRUSH corn with oil.

GRILL corn 8 to 10 min. or until tender, turning occasionally and brushing with the mustard mixture.

Who knew?

Appendix and Sources

[1] IBM Global CEO Study, 2011.

[2] *Creativity and Innovation: Key Drivers for Success,* Meisinger, Susan, HR Magazine, 2007.

[3] *PWC Breakthrough Innovation and Growth report,* 2013.

[4] Maryfran Johnson, Computerworld, September 2003. The innovation quest.

[5] *Technology Matters-Questions to live with,* Nye, David.

[6] *How Steve Jobs' Love of Simplicity Fueled A Design Revolution,* Walter Isaacson, Smithsonian, Spetember 2012.

[7] *Drive,* Pink, Daniel, 2015.

[8] Providence Talks.

[9] *Meaningful Differences in the Everyday Experience of Young American Children*, Hart, Betty, Risley Todd, 1995.

[10] *The Art of Creativity*, Goleman, Daniel, Kaufman, Paul, Ray, Michael, Publication Psychology Today, 1992.

[11] *The 7 Hidden Reasons Employees Leave: How to Recognize the Subtle Signs and Act Before It's Too Late*, Branham, Leigh, 2004.

[12] What it really takes to 'get creative' in our work, Work & Family Life 19.3 (Mar 2005): 4, Amabile, Teresa, 2005.

[13] Orbiting the Giant Hairball: A Corporate Fool's Guide to Surviving with Grace Gordon McKenzie, Viking, 1998.

[14] *Deterministic non-periodic flow*, Lorenz, Edward N., *Journal of the Atmospheric Sciences* 20 (2): 130–141, 1963.

[15] Gallup Workplace survey, 2013.

[16] *Leveraging Employee Engagement for Competitive Advantage: HR's Strategic Role*, Lockwood, Nancy R, 2007, SHRM® Research Quarterly, Publisher: Society for Human Resource Management.

[17] Publication title: *The Influence of Culture*, International Journal of Business and Management Volume: 7 Issue: 22, 2005.

[18] *The Book of Basketball*, Bill Simmons, ESPN Books, 2009.

[19] *Kirk Gibson's pinch-hit HR wins World Series game*, ESPN Sports, Rick Weinberg, June 2004.

[20] *The Checklist Manifesto*, Atul Gawande, 2009.

[21] *Atul Gawande's 'Checklist' For Surgery Success*, January 2010.

[22] *Radical Innovation Across Nations: The Preeminence of Corporate Culture*, G.J. Tellis, J.C. Prabhu and R.K. Chandy, Journal of Marketing 73, no. 1 (January 2009):3-23.

[23] *How Innovative is Your Company's Culture?* Rao and Weintraub, MIT Sloan Management Review, September 2013.

[24] *Managing With the Brain in Mind*, Rock, David, Strategy Business No. 56, 2009.

[25] *The Complex Dynamics of High Performance Teams*, Losada, Marcial, Dec 1999, *Mathematical and Computer Modelling, Vol 30.*

[26] *The topography of marital conflict: A sequential analysis of verbal and nonverbal behavior,* Marriage and *the Family 39, 461-477,* Gottman, John; Markman, Howard; Notarius, Cliff, 1977.

[27] *Patterns in chaos,* Chirikov, Boris V., *In Chaos, Order and Patterns,* (Edited by Roberto Artuso. Predrag Cvitanovic and Giulio Casati), pp. 109-134, NATO Advanced Science Institute Series, Plenum Press, 1991.

[28] *Positive organizational behavior: developing and managing psychological strengths,* Luthans, Fred, Academy of Management Executive, 16, 57-72, 2002.

[29] *The need for and meaning of positive organizational behavior* Luthans, Fred, Journal of Organizational Behavior, 2002.

[30] *Ordinary magic: resilience processes in development,* Masten, Ann S., American Psychologist, 56, 227-239, 2001.

[31] Business Week, May 2001 Sorry Steve, Cliff Edwards, May 2011.

[32] *The Apple Store at 10 past present and future,* May 2011, Gigaom.

[33] *Steve Jobs Apple and Importance Company Culture*, Julie Moreland, Fast Company.

[34] *Jon Stewart 'Crossfire' Transcript*, Stewart Slams Tucker Carlson and Paul Begala, Political humor.

[35] Congress Job Approval Starts 2014 at 13%, Jeffrey M. Jones, Gallup, January 2014.

[36] *7 Habits of Highly Effective People*, Covey, Stephen R., 1989.

[37] *In Like a Lion*, NBC-SNL 1976.

[38] *A Self-Categorization Explanation for the Hostile Media Effect*, Reid, Scott, Journal of Communication Volume 62, Issue 3, pages 381–399, June 2012.

[39] *A Cognitive Psychology of Mass Communication*, Harris, Richard Jackson, Routledge, 2009.

[40] *Red Media, Blue Media: Evidence of Ideological Selectivity in Media Use Shanto Iyengar & Kyu S. Hahn*, Journal of Communication, 2009.

[41] Average American watches 5 hours of TV per day, report shows, David Hinckley, Daily News, March 2014.

[42] *Monkey see, monkey do: The influence of work groups on the antisocial behavior of employees*, Robinson, Sandra L; O'Leary-Kelly, Anne M Publication title Academy of Management Journal, 1998.

[43] *Psychopathology in Adopted-Away Offspring of Biologic Parents with Antisocial behavior* and *Psychopathology in Adopted-Away Offspring of Biologic Parents with Antisocial behavior,* Cadoret, Remi, 35 (2): 176–184, 1978.

[44] *Social foundations of thought and action: A social cognitive theory*, Bandura, A, Englewood Cliffs, NJ: Prentice-Hall, 1986.

Social cognitive theory of moral thought and action. In W. M. Kurtines & J. L. Gewirtz (Eds.), Handbook of moral behavior and development: Theory, research, and application, Bandura, A., vol. 1: 71-129. Hillsdale, NJ: Erlbaum, 1991.

Mechanism of moral disengagement in the exercise of moral agency, Bandura, A., Barbaranelli, C., Caprara, G. V., & Pastorelli, C., Journal of Personality and Social Psychology, 71: 364-374, 1996.

[45] *A social information processing approach to job attitudes and task design,* Salancik, G. J., & Pfeffer, J., Administrative Science Quarterly, 23: 224-253, 1978.

[46] US Archives.

[47] *A two-level analysis of classroom climate in relation to social context, group composition, and organization of special support,* Allodi, M. W., Learning Environments Research, 5(3), 253–274, 2002.

[48] *Motivation and creativity: Effects of motivational orientation on creative writers,* Amabile, Teresa M. Journal of Personality and Social Psychology, 48(2), 393–397., 1985.

[49] *Fostering children's resilience,* Journal of Pediatric Nursing, 12, 21-31, Stewart, Reid, & Mangham, 1997.

[50] *Do As I Do,* Thurber, Christopher A, The Camping Magazine,76.5 (Sep/Oct 2003): 38-43.

[51] National Center for Education Statistics.

[52] *How a district ended student dropouts with personalized learning,* Roger Cook, Edsurge, April 2014.

[53] *Tony Tjan of cue ball on accepting new ideas,* Adam Bryant, New York Times, December 2012.

[54] *Cultures and Organizations: Software of the Mind,* Hofstede, Geert, *Administrative Science Quarterly* (Johnson Graduate School of Management, Cornell University) 38 (1): 132–134, March 1993.

[55] *On problem solving, Psychological Monographs,* Duncker, K., 58:5 (Whole No. 270), 1945.

[56] *Drive,* Pink, Daniel, 2011.

[57] Evaluation Apprehension, Psychology Lexicon.

[58] *Risk-Taking Culture Is Lacking in the U.S. Workplace,* Laff, Michael. T + D 61.8 (Aug 2007): 18.

[59] *Organizational Climate for Creativity and Innovation,* Ekvall, Goran, European Journal of work and organizational Psychology, 5(I),105-123, 1996.

[60] *Organizational Culture for Creativity and Innovation,* Claver, E., Llopis, J., Garcia, D., Molina, H., Venue: New Technological Behavior, Journal of High Technology Management Research, 1998.

[61] *Applied Imagination*, Osborn, Alex F., 1953.

[62] *Brainstorming groups in context: Effectiveness in a product design firm,* Sutton, Robert I; Hargadon, Andrew. Administrative Science Quarterly41.4, 685-718, December 1996.

[63] *Where good ideas come from*, Steve Johnson, TED Talks.

[64] *Where good ideas come from: The Natural History of Innovation*, Steven Johnson, October 2011.

[65] *Measuring Innovation: Gauging Your Organization's Success*, Studt, Tim. R & D47.2 42-44., February 2005.

[66] *Wearable Devices as Facilitators, Not Drivers, of Health Behavior Change,* Journal of the American Medical Association, January 2015.

[67] Edmondson, Amy (1 June 1999). "Psychological Safety and Learning Behavior in Work Teams" *Administrative Science Quarterly.* **44** (2): 350–383.

[68] *Detert, J. R.; Edmondson, A. C. (1 June 2011). "Implicit Voice Theories: Taken-for-Granted Rules of Self-Censorship at Work". Academy of Management Journal. **54** (3): 461–48*

Dysfunctional behavior in organizations, R. Griffin, A. O'Leary-Kelly, & J. Collins (Eds.), 229-240 Greenwich, CT: JAI Press.

Partisan use and perceptions of cable news programming, Coe K. Tewksbury, D., Bond, B. J., Drogos, K.L., Porter, R. W., Yahn, A., et al., Journal of Communication, 58, 201-219, 2008.

Organizational climates: An essay. Personnel Psychology, 28: 447-480. Schneider, B. 1987. The people make the place. Personnel Psychology, 40: 437-454, 1975.

The Innovation Company, LLC

www.innovationisEASY.com

978-266-0012

info@innovationisEASY.com

Workshops

Retreats

Keynotes

Management consulting

Coaching

The Innovation Company's mission and vision

Mission

The mission of The Innovation Company is to inspire individuals and organizations to create respectful, open, and innovative work environments that encourage people to constantly share and implement new ideas.

Vision

The vision of The Innovation Company is one in which all individuals, regardless of their position in the workplace or society, can present new ideas and suggestions and receive a respectful response from others that demonstrates the sincere willingness to be open to different points of views.

Printed in the United States
By Bookmasters